The President requests the several heads of Departments to take the most prudent and œconomical Arrangements for the removal of the public offices, Clerks and Papers, according to their own best Judgment as soon as may be convenient, in such manner that the public offices may be opened in the City of Washington for the dispatch of Business by the fifteenth of June

John Adams

Philadelphia
May 15ᵗʰ. 1800.

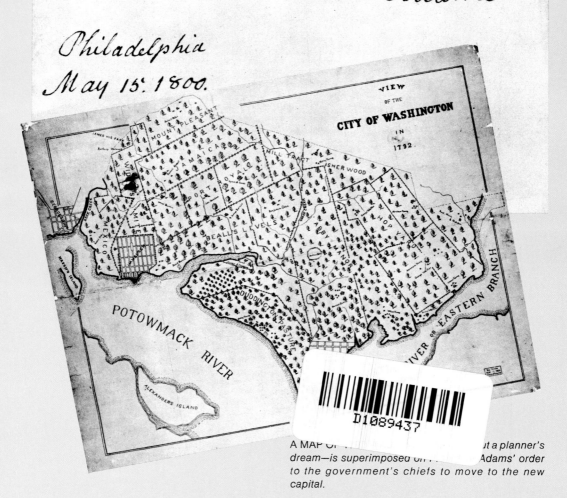

VIEW
OF THE
CITY OF WASHINGTON
IN
1792.

A MAP OF ... ut a planner's *dream—is superimposed on ... Adams' order to the government's chiefs to move to the new capital.*

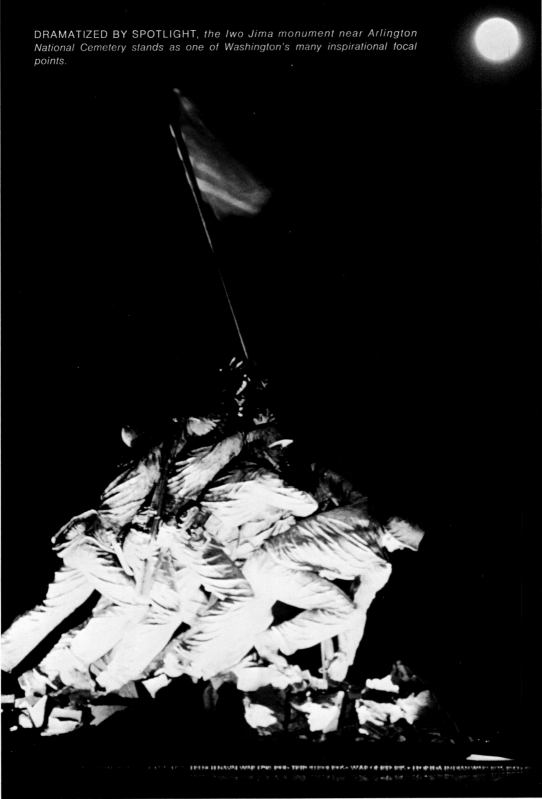

DRAMATIZED BY SPOTLIGHT, *the Iwo Jima monument near Arlington National Cemetery stands as one of Washington's many inspirational focal points.*

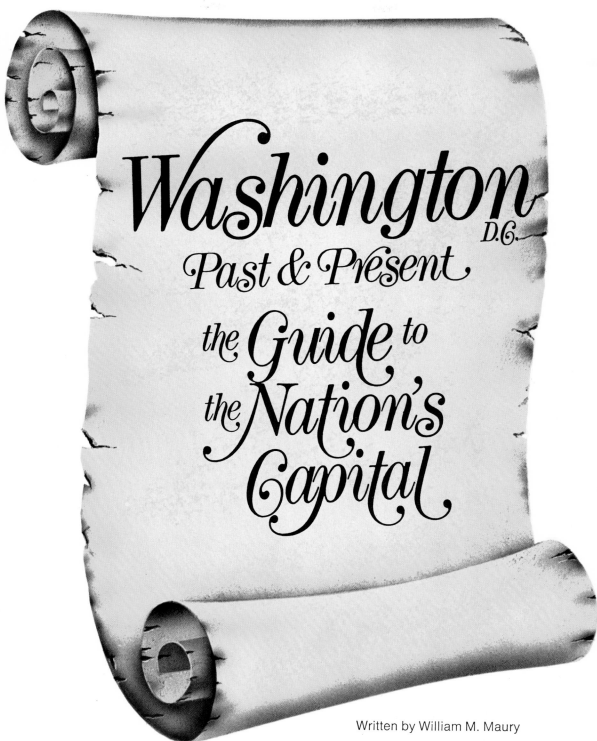

Washington D.C.

Past & Present

the Guide to the Nation's Capital

Written by William M. Maury

Published by CBS Publications, New York City, in cooperation with the United States Capitol Historical Society
Library of Congress Catalog Number 74-25430   All Rights Reserved   Printed in the United States of America

Introduction

A century ago, Frederick Douglass called Washington, D.C., "the most luminous point of American territory; a city recently transformed and made beautiful in its body and in its spirit." He spoke at the unveiling of the Freedman's Monument in Lincoln Park. He was moved not only by the capital's spiritual transformation in the wake of slavery's abolition, but also by its physical transformation in anticipation of the Centennial. Nevertheless, the physical reality of Washington in 1876 presents a stark contrast to the Washington of the Bicentennial.

As this book reveals, the city evolved slowly and painfully from the raw and graceless town that Dickens decried in 1844 as the "city of Magnificent Intentions." For much of its history, it was dirty and discomforting; its few aesthetically pleasing buildings and monuments served as a contrast which emphasized the surrounding blight.

When Lincoln came to Washington from Illinois, in 1861, only a few scattered buildings lay in the swamp between the Executive Mansion and Capitol Hill, and the unfinished stub of the Washington Monument rose in a pasture where cattle grazed. The domeless Capitol and the half-built Monument were twin symbols of the unfinished agenda of a young nation embarked on a difficult journey — an experiment in self-government — begun a century earlier. Scattered boarding-houses, hotels, markets and stores along Pennsylvania Avenue, then a drab cere-monial boulevard, faced the Capitol. First a creek and then a canal flowed between the White House and what is now one of the noblest spires in the world. The canal has long since been replaced by stately Constitution Avenue, traveled daily by masses of residents, commuters and visitors.

So dreadful was the combination of dust, swamp, and mosquitos that in July and August, Lincoln used the Old Soldiers Home on Rock Creek Church Road at Upshur Street as a "summer White House," while the nation was locked in the most savage war in all history. Union soldiers faced Confederate troops whose lines often ran to the Virginia side of Chain Bridge, just beyond Georgetown.

Behind Lincoln's determination to complete the dome of the Capitol was his sure knowledge that "we live by symbols," as Mr. Justice Holmes later observed. Even as the dome moved toward completion, it was a symbol of the unity that Lincoln struggled to preserve. From the west entrance of the Capitol, one can stand today and see below the bronze figure of the great Chief Justice, John Marshall. Beyond is the new reflecting pool, and a mile away the Washington Monument, not completed until 1884.

Visitors to the nation's capital might think that the city was born beautiful, since it focuses on memorials to Presidents and military heroes, a maze of statuary, parks large and small, and great public buildings, especially the White House, the Capitol and the Supreme Court.

It would be impossible to catalog all the great events that have taken place within the Capitol's marble walls, but any list would include the great debates in Congress when Daniel Webster, Henry Clay, and John Calhoun held their colleagues spellbound. It would include landmark decisions of the Supreme Court, delivered by its Justices from early cramped quarters in the basement, and later from the impressive room beside the present Senate Chamber — before the Court was appropriately housed, in 1935, in its present magnificent building.

Within the Capitol's walls, great leaders of this century have given accounts of stewardship or exhorted Americans to unity and struggle — Wilson, "F.D.R.," Churchill, de Gaulle and Generals MacArthur and Eisenhower, to name a few. And who knows, perhaps the unfolding developments of this decade will bring the leaders of the Soviet Union and the Chinese People's Republic to these same halls to manifest their agreement that this is truly one world which we must share with each other if peace is to survive.

This book traces the capital's jagged and often turbulent development from its feeble beginning to the public magnificence that we enjoy today. While we take pride in the beauty of the public Washington, we cannot forget "the other Washington" where hovels and tenements still survive. The Washington of today is still the Washington of yesteryear for those of its people who suffer the blight of poverty and of inner-city crime. We hope that in time we can be as proud of the "private Washington" as we are today of the public Washington, making the city a full embodiment over means and methods, but united in the never-ending quest for liberty, equal opportunity and equal justice under law.

Warren E. Burger

The Chief Justice,
United States Supreme Court

Contents

Foreword

The City of Washington is an inspiration to people from all over the world. The memorials here, said one distinguished visitor, ''are the real temples to which each generation must pay tribute and in doing so, catch something of the fire that burned in the hearts of those who were the torch-bearers of freedom, not only for this country but for the world.''

The United States Capitol Historical Society, in cooperation with the CBS Publishing Group, presents this book in the hope that with it, visitors and potential visitors to Washington will more fully understand and appreciate this great capital city.

The book contains more than 200 illustrations, selected from public and private collections to document the city's growth. The text covers the full history of the city in a highly readable fashion that includes many fascinating historical anecdotes. Both text and pictures have been carefully scrutinized by highly qualified experts on Washington.

Full of interesting insights into the history of America, this book is first and foremost about Washington, D.C. Built for those who govern, this city has been the central stage of America's dramatic past and is the take-off point for her challenging future. The story of the capital's creation ''like that of the nation itself, was one of daring experiment and noble compromise, salted with acts of greed and deceit.'' That statement will be appreciated by all who understand our nation's early hard beginnings and it is important that we understand them. As Carl Sandburg once said, ''Whenever a people or an institution forgets its early hard beginnings it is beginning to decay.'' Our book was prepared with the objective of helping us to remember some of our early hard beginnings and encouraging us to learn more.

''Washington, Past and Present'' in a single volume has more interesting and worthwhile information than can be found in any book about the capital area. The authors and publishers of the several prestigious books about the capital's institutions will welcome this new and needed display of history. These books will become a beautiful ''Tableau of the Capital.''

This book contains many illustrations not available in any other publication along with enough information to satisfy the interests of avid historians. The visitor to our nation's capital city will be proud to have it as a valuable addition to his library.

Fred Schwengel

Fred Schwengel
President, U.S. Capitol Historical Society

The City That History Made

Preamble

Washington: At once a mecca for Americans and a mirror of America.

It was trackless marsh and meadows when the nation was conceived in 1776, and a frontier village when the infant United States crawled west. Today it is the hub of a metropolis embracing 2.5 million Americans.

Built for those who govern, this city has been the central stage of America's dramatic past — and is the take-off point of her challenging future. Scene of exuberant parades when harmonious pride eclipses differences, the capital also bears scars from the burning disappointments of other years. It is a city freshened by a hundred flowering parks, and darkened by some scattered slums.

Its streets are often jammed — with civil servants, with football traffic, with tourists and shoppers browsing through sidewalk vendors' wares, with flag-waving partisans and ribboned diplomats crowding a Presidential inaugural.

Down from the Capitol, the Mall bursts its bounds each July with a Folk Festival that celebrates America, from aging Appalachian dulcimer makers to brawny union men showing how to build skyscraping skeletons of steel. Yet on other occasions, after marchers have walked in step to petition their government for their birthrights and then gone home to Massachusetts or across the Mississippi, this expansive greensward may be suddenly silent and empty and pristinely beautiful.

Here marble monuments recall history's heroes, while modern men breathe the life of legislation into present-day realities. Both a living city and a cloister of pillared memorials, it is home for 750,000 of us and a place to visit for 18 million more each year: Foreign tourists curious to see the seat of the Western World's mightiest power . . . Schools of students to witness the working government they've studied . . . Vacationing families of polo-shirted pilgrims to view the capital of their republic . . . Symphony buffs, gourmets and antique airplane fans . . . People whose private business brings them to challenge or cajole public officials . . . Scholars and scoundrels, demonstrators and Daughters of the American Revolution. Scientists, sychophants, supplicants and sunbathers — all are drawn to this place where life is harnessed by historical habits and spurred by changing national goals.

Dynamic, monumental, political, imperfect — both historical and forward-looking — it is your capital and mine, our city and shrine.

Welcome.

ON THE STEPS OF THE CAPITOL *an honor guard of all the armed services marshals the colors.*

YESTERDAY THE REFLECTING POOL *gave young people a chance to take a dip and show off their boat models at the foot of the Lincoln Memorial.*

TODAY THE REFLECTING POOL, *which graces the Mall along the capital's main axis, still offers citizens and visitors a refreshing and social meeting place.*

MOODS OF THE MALL *range from tails to t-shirts. By morning and noontime joggers charge around the reflecting pool's borders; in the afternoon a symphony orchestra may have materialized to celebrate a grand occasion; at dusk the fountains glimmer in the fading light beneath the Lincoln Memorial.*

The very complexity of the nation we now know contributes to Washington's status as its most important city. New York's stock market rumblings can mean bad business in Tuscaloosa or even Tokyo; Oakland may monopolize the nation's attention for a World Series and New Orleans is still the "Queen City of the South." But it is Washington that symbolizes America throughout the world. Day in and day out she touches the life of every American with her deeds and declarations. For better or worse, the trend of the past forty years has been to involve government in more aspects of everyday life. So every street and backwater across the land feels the impact of words spoken and written here: the warnings or promises of a Presidential message; the text of a new law passed by Congress; a Supreme Court ruling that strives to keep the promise of "equal justice under law" for all Americans.

(continued on page 17)

A TWO-LEVEL ARCHWAY *leads from the great hall to the Main Reading room (lower) and the Library's vast interior spaces. The structure, designed by Smithmeyer and Pelz, was completed in 1897.*

SPORTING IN THE FOUNTAIN, *Neptune's Court (left) decorates the west facade of the ornate Library (below). If the god stepped down from his steed, he would stand 12 feet tall.*

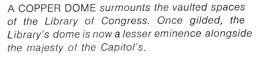

A COPPER DOME *surmounts the vaulted spaces of the Library of Congress. Once gilded, the Library's dome is now a lesser eminence alongside the majesty of the Capitol's.*

THE MAIN READING ROOM of the Library of Congress is pictured in the "fisheye" shot above. The eight-sided room features three different colors of richly veined marble. The glorious painting on the dome's collar is by Edward Blashfield.

GAZING INTO THE FUTURE, the statue of Commerce, one of eight allegorical figures which adorn the uppermost level of the Main Reading Room, holds a locomotive engine in her left hand and a ship in her right. Sculpted by John F. Flanagan, she is seen at right just before being put in place.

Capitol Hill

When Pierre L'Enfant first saw Capitol Hill in its natural form he called it "a pedestal awaiting a monument." But it was decades before the Hill's destiny began to be fulfilled. The Capitol, designed by William Thornton, was the first public building, opening its doors in 1800. The present dome and wings for the two houses of Congress were designed by Thomas U. Walter a half-century later. At first, the Capitol served as a catch-all for governmental agencies on the Hill.

The Library of Congress was housed in the Capitol until 1897, when the main building, designed by John C. Smithmeyer and Paul J. Pelz, was completed. With the annex, completed in 1939, and the new Madison addition to be completed in 1977, the Library is the largest in the world, containing 17,000,000 books and pamphlets, 72,000,000 total pieces. It also has a large collection of Stradivarius instruments which are played by the Library's resident quartet, the Julliard.

Until the beginning of this century, Congressmen vied with one another for office space in the Capitol. Then the Cannon House Office Building and the Russell Senate Office Building were constructed. Designed by architects Robert Carrere and Thomas Hastings, the buildings are nearly identical and are found respectively on the south and north flanks of the Capitol. In 1933, the Longworth House Office Building, designed by John Harveson, William Hough and William Livingston, further eased the crush. After WW II further space was allotted with the completion in 1958 of the Dirksen Senate Office Building, designed by Otto Eggers and Daniel Higgins, and the 1965 completion of the Rayburn House Office Building, designed by Roy Lamar.

Until 1935, the Capitol also served as the home of the Supreme Court. When Cass Gilbert's austere neo-classical structure was finally completed, one justice remarked that in it the justices would look like "nine black beetles in the temple of Karnak." Nearly square, the building also houses a 200,000 volume library.

Across second street from the Supreme Court is the famed Folger Library. Designed by Paul Cret and Alexander Trowbridge, it was built with private funds to house the Shakespeare collection of Henry Clay Folger. Probably the largest library strictly devoted to the age of Shakespeare, the building includes a stage built in the theater style of Elizabethan England.

About seven blocks east of the Folger is Eastern Market. Designed by Adolf Cluss and completed in 1872, it is one of the last remaining vestiges of the city's once extensive municipally run market system. Eastern Market offers diversity for shoppers and a quiet retreat into the 19th century. A few blocks away, on 8th and I Streets, stands the home of the Commandant of the Marine Corps. Built in 1806, the home is the oldest continuously occupied government building in the city. It overlooks the parade grounds of the Marine Barracks, the scene of retreat parades on Friday evenings in the summer.

At the base of Capitol Hill is the always fragrant Botanical Garden Building. Designed by the architectural team of Bennett, Parsons and Frost and completed in 1932, it includes species of plants from all over the United States. These tightly grouped sights plus numerous restored 19th and 20th century townhouses make a tour of Capitol Hill rewarding for the visitor.

MEETING IN JOINT ASSEMBLY, *the two branches of Congress convene in the House's South Wing when grand occasions call them together (above). Sharing the crest of the Hill with them is the Supreme Court building (below).*

VIEWING THE CAPITOL WITH AWE, *a statue of Shakespeare's Puck kneels in front of the Folger Library. The Folger is one of several cultural institutions which the visitor to the Hill finds waiting for him and his family.* Ⓖ

SIGHTSEERS *at the White House in this 1889 shot seem equally amazed at the President's mansion and the marvels of the then-new portable camera.*

TOURISTS AND PETITIONERS *have flocked to the capital since its inception. These include the rotunda visitors shown below from the Reconstruction era and the "tin lizzie" campers above, as well as the Japanese maidens by the tidal pool at right. One never knows what one may see: even a frozen memorial to explorer Robert Peary (below, right).*

(continued from page 12)

Government has always been to Washington what steel is to Pittsburgh, what steak is to Kansas City, what make-believe is to Hollywood. If the modern world's first democracy had not been established, this city would never have been founded. Unlike Paris, London or Rome, it did not emerge as the capital because it was a nascent nation's preeminent city; Washington became a city in the first place because it was to be the capital. America's first leaders were inventing a new form of government for the world; as its seat they also planned a city from the ground up. Rather than a city for the common man, the city they planned would rival Versailles, the French stronghold of the aristocracy. Like the nation it led, the city of marble and macadam is the realization of a dream — an ideal that has been bent and stretched to suit the changing realities of different times.

The city grew in step with the republic. Each national crisis and every victory left its mark on Washington. As the nation grew in territory and population, so did the activities of government; as the government grew, so did the city. In 1801 some 130 people held government jobs. That figure has swelled to nearly 400,000 in the metropolitan area alone. New federal employees trickled in during the quiet years and flooded the city by trainloads during times of national emergency. Consequently, both government and city seem orderly and well-planned in places; elsewhere there is chaos that can confuse even a native bureaucrat.

HOLIDAYS AND DEMONSTRATIONS *draw the people of the U.S. to Washington to climb the Capitol's West front stairway, to see the beauty of the Washington spring (below, left), to celebrate an inaugural (above), or to plea for "human kindness" (below).*

Washington is where decisions that affect everyone are made: by the Agriculture Department to raise grain prices; by the Federal Reserve Board to increase interest rates; by the Surgeon General to try curing the common cold; by the Senate to approve a disarmament treaty; by the President to send combat-ready Marines overseas; by the Interior Department to preserve an open beach as national parkland; by the Ways and Means Committee to vote a tax bill; by the Office of Emergency Preparedness to stockpile life-saving supplies against rampaging tornadoes.

Such matters are Washington's stock in trade because they are the daily business of government, which is nothing more or less than the conduct of the people's business. That's politics: different officials who represent divergent viewpoints thrashing out national plans and policies. (Some visitors say they detest politics while honoring history. But history, after all, is in part the remembered course of past political events, with many of the painful problems and personal dilemmas blurred by time or choice. When the colonists decided to overthrow their legal government, they acted politically and risked death for their actions. History calls them "founding fathers." King George III called them rebels. What we recall as heroic was, for them, the very risky business of political life in troubled times.)

Fittingly, the site of this most political of all cities was decided upon by an act of political compromise. (See page 38) Ever since George Washington bent that early agreement to suit his own purposes, the city has been shaped by political events and the many-faceted personalities of men like John C. Calhoun, Charles Sumner, Robert LaFollette, and Sam Rayburn. Neither total bums nor total heroes, those who have directed the city's course have been real people with individual ambitions, appetites and foibles as well as strengths. They coped with agonizing problems and acid-tongued adversaries to build the city and the nation.

Thus Washington's shape and face have changed to answer history's challenges of expansion, war, depression and peace. Streets and circles designed for the slow-

GOING TO AND FROM WASHINGTON, *an Indian chief is satirized in the painting at left. Artist George Catlin may also have been satirizing the government itself and its treatment of the Indians.*

TEPEES IN THE CAPITAL *(opposite, at right below) can be seen by visitors to the Folk Festival, held each year on the Mall by the Smithsonian Institution. Other scenes recall feathered headdresses from earlier years (clockwise); after the Civil War, with President Harding, and at a Shrine Convention.*

paced trot of horses now bear the traffic of vehicles undreamt of by eighteenth century planners. Wide streets glutted with traffic have hurried the coming of Metro, a 98-mile subway system that, when completed, will be the largest single public works project in U.S. history. The city has even adapted its shape to fit the realities of government. Originally a perfect square straddling the Potomac, the Virginia portion (on the other side of the Potomac from the larger Maryland portion) proved hard to govern, and so was returned to the ''Old Dominion'' in 1846. Congress has recognized this organic ability of the city to change, and in recent years has granted increased rights of self-government to Washingtonians (though Congress still rules here as ''master in its own house'').

During the early decades, Washington was unpopular among people whose official duties required their presence. Congressmen stayed as briefly as the short legislative sessions demanded. Most left their families at home rather than expose them to the marshy region's ''miasmic vapors,'' and lived in boarding houses like political fraternity brothers. Many stayed only for one term — the biennial turnover in the House of Representatives was around 50 percent. For foreign ambassadors, early Washington was a hardship post. A British diplomat sarcastically observed in 1820: ''In the present state of this celebrated metropolis, the life of a foreigner must ever be one of privation and restraint.''

Despite all this, citizens were drawn to the seat of government because it was the place of power. Some came to exercise that power as elected representatives, as appointed officials, as career civil servants. Others, especially in this century, came to see and learn. But since the earliest years, the most visible visitors have been people journeying here in the name of a cause.

The first petitioners were Indians who brightened the scene with their native dress as they came to verify treaties that were often broken. (One of the most colorful funeral processions ever seen here followed the bier of Choctaw Chief Push-ma-ta-ha to Congressional Cemetery above the Potomac's eastern branch, known as the Anacostia River.) In 1894 ''Coxey's Army''
(continued on page 26)

G

G

I

J

Culture
In The Capital

From a wilderness, Washington has become a cultural oasis. Much of Washington's culture is institutional and government supported. But much is also innovative and private.

Among the private galleries three varied examples stand out. The Phillips Gallery at the corner of 21st and P Streets, N.W. displays one of the nation's largest privately collected 19th and 20th century art treasures. The main gallery is an attractive restored brownstone designed by architects Hornblower and Marshall. There is, in addition, a modern wing built in 1960. Most of the collection was amassed by Duncan Phillips, who lived in the mansion until 1930. The gallery also features solo and chamber music on Sunday afternoons during the season. The Museum of African Art is located in the Grant-era house on A Street between 3rd and 4th Streets, N.E., which was occupied by Frederick Douglass until 1877. It was opened as a museum in 1964 and has on display over 500 pieces of African Art, both contemporary and historic. The Corcoran Gallery, at the corner of 17th and E Streets, N.W. built in 1897, is the oldest private gallery in the city. Architect Ernest Flagg's commodious building houses a collection of mostly American art from the 18th, 19th and 20th centuries.

Music flourishes in Washington, whether it's privately or publicly funded. The 96-member National Symphony Orchestra plays a 200-performance schedule of music ranging from the classical to pops; the 43-year old National is the resident orchestra of the Kennedy Center for the Performing Arts, and is now directed by Maestro Anatol Dorati. The Filene Center at Wolf Trap Farm, just off the Dulles Airport access road, offers a wide range of music all summer long in a handsome indoor-outdoor setting designed by John MacFadgen and Edward Knowles and completed in 1971. The Carter Barron Amphitheatre, near 16th and Kennedy Streets, N.W. built in 1950 by the National Park Service, provides pleasant surroundings for outdoor concerts of modern, popular music. Concerts by the U.S. Marine Band have been part of Washington since 1801. In the past 52 years the Army, the Navy and Air Force have also developed bands which play at the Jefferson Memorial and the Capitol Plaza six nights a week.

For those who like the legitimate stage there are several thriving theatres in Washington. The historic National Theatre on Pennsylvania Avenue and 13th Street, N.W. dauntlessly carries on in a structure which includes portions of the original 1835 building; other portions have been claimed by fire. The Arena/Kreeger complex in new Southwest Washington, offers repertory theatre to Washington residents. The Arena, a theatre-in-the-round designed by Harry Weese, was built in 1961, the Kreeger, also designed by Weese, was completed in 1971. Together the theatres produce about eight plays a year, ranging in style from the classical to the very modern. Ford's Theatre, on 10th Street, N.W. (site of Lincoln's assassination), was built in 1863 and reopened by the Park Service in 1966. Ford's specializes in musicals, and includes a small but very interesting Lincoln museum on the lower floor. In the small Maryland town of Olney, out Georgia Avenue extended, audiences are delighted all summer by summer stock productions of high quality in very pleasant surroundings.

Added to these bright lights and silver curtains are several night clubs that feature star-quality performers. With Washington's numerous movie theatres and gala openings, there is surely something for everyone every night in the capital.

A VARIETY OF PERFORMING ARTS *have turned Washington's plazas into noontime concert halls (right) and its citizens into first-nighters.*

A NATIONAL PARK FOR PERFORMING ARTS *Wolf Trap Farm (below) draws Washingtonians to the Virginia countryside for indoor and outdoor enjoyment.*

G   G

THE KENNEDY CENTER *a gleaming box which houses three separate performance halls, sits on the Potomac's bank (below). The bust of President Kennedy is by Robert Berkes.*

G   G

WITH A FLURRY OF COLORS, *Washington's "Old Guard"—the first battalion of the Third Infantry Division, stationed at Fort Meyer* stages a dazzling display (left and below) for visitors to the Jefferson Memorial every Wednesday evening during the summer.

G

POMP AND CEREMONY *mark important moments on Washington's calendar of events throughout the years.*

G

WITH MUFFLED DRUMS *the city marked the passing of President Lyndon Johnson's funeral caisson.*

THE WASHINGTON MONUMENT *is the scene of a salute to the birthday of the nation's first President.*

HISTORIC GEORGETOWN, *seen as a port city on the western fringe of the capital on the 1800 "handkerchief map" above, was called a city without streets, while Washington was a city of streets without houses.*

TODAY'S GEORGETOWN *offers a mix of shops to visitors of all tastes and styles—everything from the fashionably scruffy to the elegantly chaste.*

FAMOUS AMERICANS *lived behind the doorways of Georgetown's gracious homes (right). Francis Scott Key's home, which stood on M Street at the present site of Key Bridge, is recalled in the painting above.*

(continued from page 19)

of unemployed entered the city 400 strong to seek public assistance and jobs. They were met with billy clubs and arrested for walking on the grass below the Capitol, whose dome Lincoln ordered completed during the war that ended slavery. In 1932, when the Great Depression was deepening, the "Bonus Army" of World War I veterans camped in Anacostia until cavalry troops drove them away with tear gas and bayonets. Over the years women have marched down Pennsylvania Avenue to demand the vote and hooded Ku Klux Klansmen have paraded for bigotry. In 1945 General Eisenhower led victorious fighting men along the avenue in a celebration that the entire nation applauded. Eighteen years later the doleful drums of martyred John Kennedy's cortege echoed mourning hearts across the continent and around the world.

The largest gathering in history bore witness here against the Vietnam war. But perhaps the most inspiring single demonstration was the civil rights march led by the Rev. Dr. Martin Luther King, Jr. On August 28, 1963, 200,000 people gathered at the foot of the Lincoln Memorial and along the Reflecting Pool to affirm their belief in the unfulfilled promise that "all men are created equal" whether born black or white. Dr. King declared "I have a dream . . ." and for a time it seemed the nation shared it. Five years later blacks in Washington and other cities spontaneously exploded in flaming riots when King was murdered. His dream of harmony is yet to be fulfilled.

(continued on page 32)

LET'S PICK UP A GAME! *say boys with hockey sticks and a yen to play on the frozen C & O canal above Georgetown.*

LET'S STAY IN WASHINGTON, *say occupants of successful renewal projects such as the New-town Center (below), who decline to be banished from their city by the ever-growing structures for government and commerce.*

Places of Historical Interest

Famous and infamous, Washington is home to people from all walks of life. Politicians and diplomats live cheek by jowl with writers and inventors, musicians and conspirators.

Lafayette Park, directly across from the north front of the White House was an early center of society in Washington. The Decatur House, at the corner of Jackson Place and H Streets, N.W. (now a naval museum specializing in early 19th and post-civil war naval artifacts) was the home of Stephen Decatur, the naval hero, who coined the phrase "My country right or wrong" and was later killed in a duel. Across Lafayette Park from the Decatur House, on the corner of H and Madison Place, is the house where James and Dolley Madison lived for many years after leaving the White House in 1821. Dolley, a society leader to the end, died there in 1849.

Nearby; on the corner of 15th and F Streets, stands Rhode's Tavern. One of the oldest commercial buildings in the city, it was home to some congressmen, and was used by the British command during the burning of Washington in 1814. Several blocks away, at 516 10th Street, is the simple Petersen House where President Lincoln died. About seven blocks away, at 627 Pennsylvania Avenue, the second floor of the Weiss Camera Shop was the studio of Civil War photographer Mathew Brady known for his Lincoln portraits.

Southeast Washington has several interesting homes including that of Thomas Tingy in the Navy Yard. Tingy commanded that post during the War of 1812. At 14th and W Streets S.E. stands the mid-Victorian mansion Cedar Hill, long the residence of Frederick Douglass, the great black orator and civil-libertarian.

Meridian Hill and Mount Pleasant, N.W. were home to several renowned Americans including the great jazzman and composer Edward "Duke" Ellington and America's first lady of the theatre, Helen Hayes, who lived at 1212 T Street and at 12th and T Streets, respectively. Alexander Graham Bell made his home at 1500 Rhode Island Avenue, N.W. just above Thomas Circle, and the Surratt house, where much of the Lincoln assassination plot was developed, is now a Chinese market at 604 H Street, N.W.

The Dupont Circle area also boasts several historic homes. Sinclair Lewis, the author of *Babbit* and *Main Street* among many other novels of American life, lived for awhile in the little house at 1635 19th Street, N.W. Not far away, at the corner of P and 21st Streets stands the Moroccan Embassy, once the home of Under Secretary of the Navy, later President, Theodore Roosevelt. One of the most interesting homes in the area is the mansion now occupied by the Columbia Historical Society; it was built by one of the city's largest beer makers, Christian Heurich.

In Georgetown, the old Stone House, one one can stroll among several interesting homes. The so-called "Marshall House" at 1801 F Street, N.W. has been occupied by Presidents Madison and Van Buren, Civil War General George McClellan and Justice John Marshall in its long life. At 2017 I Street stands the Arts Club of Washington, once the home of President James Monroe.

In The George Washington University area of the oldest structures in the city at 3051 M Street, was supposedly L'Enfant's headquarters when he laid out the capital city. At 3400 Prospect Avenue Benjamin Stoddart, the first Secretary of the Navy, built his home to overlook Georgetown's waterfront. Dumbarton Oaks at 3101 R Street, scene of the important WW II meeting, overlooks rustic Montrose Park.

Walking or driving past these houses, particularly at night, one senses the spirits of Washington past commingling and concurring that this is a fascinating place to live in as well as visit.

HOUSING VIP'S, *Blair House (left)* extends a green awning and a gracious welcome to visitors. It stands across Pennsylvania Avenue from the White House.

WATCHING VIP'S *is a favorite sport in Washington. At left the grande dame of Washington society, Alice Roosevelt Longworth is spotted in a crowd. On the inaugural platform below, VIP's strain to catch glimpses of each other.*

"FREEDOM SHRIEK'D *As Kosciuszko Fell!*" is inscribed on the statue of the Polish hero of the American Revolution (right) which stands on the northeast corner of Lafayette Square.

HEROES OF OTHER COUNTRIES *are memorialized in many of Washington's parks and squares. Simon Bolivar, known as "The Liberator" in South America is represented below.*

OUTDOOR WORKS OF ART of architecture and sculpture make Washington a mecca for art lovers. At left, the intriguing piece "Balance" arrests the eye of all who visit the Corcoran Gallery. Constantino Nivola's evocative memorial to the Four Chaplains stands near the George Washington Memorial Parkway in Fairfax, Virginia (below). Mies Van de Rohe's design for the new Martin Luther King Library (top) lends strength and dignity to downtown clutter.

(continued from page 26)

Nonetheless, when Americans have something to cheer about, they flock to Washington to celebrate. When they have a fallen hero to mourn, it is on these streets they spend their grief. When they believe their government is misguided, they marshal here shoulder to shoulder — because within these buildings abides the power to change events. And, while that power is held in stewardship by relatively few elected officials, it is influenced by uncounted hands and heads — by the press, by groups of people united in some common interest, by individuals depending on the pure strength of moral personality. There are 100 U.S. Senators, and ten times that many journalists entitled to witness their debates from the press gallery. There are 435 men and women in the House of Representatives, but thousands of registered lobbyists, professionals paid to represent the special interests of corporations, church groups, conservationists, cotton planters and thousands more. The Justice Department employs 2,000 attorneys, but the telephone book lists 18 small-print pages of lawyers — a few of whom argue before the Supreme Court while many more influence the nation by practicing general law in the busy metropolitan area.

This points up a curious fact of Washington life: while the city grew around government, it also evolved a day-to-day life of its own. Many people here have only the slimmest official connection with government, but they sell groceries to Senators' wives and deliver their mail, they treat ambassadors' backaches and taxi constituents from the airports to Capitol Hill offices; they teach school, direct traffic, sell insurance, run art galleries, stage plays, sell real estate, write books, restore houses and do the things that people do everywhere. The homely commonplaces of our town involve folks who are famous elsewhere as well as their friends who may be unknown outside the neighborhood. On Queen Elizabeth's birthday,

PENNSYLVANIA AVENUE *stretches from the Capitol (background in photo at left) past the White House. Here the Presidents of our nation pass in review on their inauguration days, accompanied by the tramp of uniformed escorts.*

THE GRAND ZIG-ZAG *occurs when Pennsylvania Avenue swings around the Treasury Building at 15th Street (foreground in photo opposite). Here all parades must regroup because the building's bulk intrudes itself upon the ceremonial avenue.*

homebound commuters curse Massachusetts Avenue clogged with limousines taking distinguished guests to a champagne party at the British Embassy. Those ladies sitting near you — in a movie, a restaurant, at the Kennedy Center — may be the wives of Cabinet Secretaries. The jogger running down Connecticut Avenue in the early morning is likely to be a Senator, and the hiker on the Chesapeake and Ohio Canal Towpath might easily be a Supreme Court Justice, while the guy going to work on ''the Hill'' may be a pharmacist or historian.

So be sure to keep your eyes peeled — and not only for reminders of the people and events that changed the nation's course in the years past. Take time to walk about the city. Look up at the dated pediments of buildings and read the innumerable brass plaques that recall chapters of tomorrow's prologue. Study the thousand statues, and relax beside the small memorial fountains. There is history all around you, as well as people who will live in your grandchildren's history books.

You'll certainly see the celebrated sights: the Capitol, the White House, Arlington National Cemetary and the Mall with its famed reminders of Washington, Jefferson and Lincoln and the fascinating Smithsonian Institution museums. But don't neglect the less-heralded places: lively Dupont Circle with its bookstores, restored mansions and chess players; the busy shopping district on F Street; the ''New Southwest'' with its waterfront shellfish stands, its planned communities of highrises and row houses and world-famous Arena Stage; Georgetown with its shaded brick sidewalks and Federal Era homes; Rock Creek Park with its Zoo and picnic sites; Cleveland Park with its rambling victorian houses and spacious lawns. These are the places where Washingtonians live and play — the people charged with running your government.

It is a lively, graceful, varied city. Be proud of it.

The Birth of A City

When the United States came into being under the Constitution, this city did not exist. The place we now know as Washington, D.C. was an expanse of swamps, fields, forests, orchards and stone quarries that Indians had used for centuries. The story of the capital's creation — like that of the nation itself — is one of daring experiment and noble compromise, salted with acts of greed and deceit. In the 1780's hope abounded on both sides of the Atlantic for a form of government new to the world, a hybrid flowering of Europe's Age of Reason. But governments are made of laws and men; cities of men and stones. The building of either was no certain process with a guaranteed outcome. Yet, irregularly, both city and government were built and have remained nearly two centuries—chinked mortar, charred lintels, out-of-plumb walls, crooked streets and all.

DOWN THE POTOMAC *an artist about 1800 depicted a rural scene, with the capital yet to be built.*

On April 30, 1789 George Washington took the helm of the new American ship of state. It was a time of hope and great excitement, but it was a time of crisis as well. The Constitution would not be worth the parchment it was engrossed on if the new government could not bring unity to the once separate and independent colonies. During the Revolutionary War, during the Confederation Period that followed, and even during the contest for ratification of the Constitution, the states had operated as separate entities. The people who lived in the small communities up and down the coast thought of their states almost as we now think of our nation. They identified themselves as Virginians, New Yorkers, or Georgians — only secondarily did they consider themselves Americans. The Articles of Confederation, drawn with care, emphasized the states' supremacy over the federal government. As a philosophical document, the Articles were thought-provoking, as the charter for a government, they seemed unworkable. George Washington believed that the Articles led to "internal dissentions, and jarrings with our neighbours" and "lessen[ed] our national character and importance in the eyes of European powers."

The Constitution was drafted to correct the Articles' apparent shortcomings by creating a strong central government, which many framers considered a necessary evil at best. After much debate in print and in person, after many manueverings and compromises the new document was ratified by eleven states. Washington's election, six years after the British agreed to the independence we had claimed seven years before, consummated the marriage of our nation to the Constitution and a new form of centralized government.

(continued on page 37)

UPON THE HILL *the Capitol gradually grew. This early watercolor shows a wooden walkway between the two wings.*

G

35

Washington
and
Other World Capitals

Washington was laid out when city planning was first gaining popularity in Europe. Pierre L'Enfant, appointed to design the American capital, sought to apply these early concepts to the design for the city he wanted to call "Washingtonople." He studied the designs of several new European cities as well as plans for proposed changes in older cities.

L'Enfant saw the Potomac River as serving Washington as the Seine did Paris or the Thames London. And in his mind's eye he pictured forests giving way to broad avenues radiating from central plazas like those in Rome. These wide radial boulevards would lend themselves to noble vistas, and in a more practical sense, allow for easier crowd control on ceremonial occasions. Throughout the city L'Enfant hoped that balance and symmetry would lend an aura of reason to a city where this virtue would be greatly needed.

Almost from the first L'Enfant's classic dream ran afoul of harsh realities. No plans for the President's House called for it to be of sufficient size to counter-balance the massive Capitol at the other end of Pennsylvania Avenue, and the Treasury Building soon blocked the majestic progress of this major ceremonial avenue. As time passed further violence was done to L'Enfant's classic plan. The planned formal mall became a vast train yard and the radial avenues, rather than allowing for beautiful vistas, often broke the city into little uncoordinated segments. For architects and city planners the ugliness of the capital was appalling.

At the beginning of the 20th century the country was swept at long last with a desire to beautify its cities. Washington was to be the chief example of beautification, and once again the grand pattern of European cities would be followed. Yet progress was spotty; only after more delays were the tracks removed from the mall and a graceful new station built.

But even with concepts of European magnificence in the backs of the planners' minds, Washington retained its American style. Offices and shops and taverns snuggled in where they were never supposed to be. Also the very fact that it was planned as a new center for government precluded the possibility of disrupting the pattern with old, crooked streets as in London, or of retaining a state within a city as in Rome. Washington would be a unique city.

So our capital, as the country it leads, has borrowed heavily from the old world in its construction. But the ideas have been refined to fit our own style. L'Enfant would, perhaps, be horrified but here Americans feel at home.

G

36

(continued from page 35)

In a sense, the nation's center was focused on one man, Washington, whose election had been inevitable. A popular war hero, a towering robust man of 6 feet 2 inches and 200 pounds, he was much more imposing than his surviving portraits show. Before marrying the wealthy widow Martha Custis, he had surveyed trackless wildernesses, fought Frenchmen and Indians, rafted down rivers in flood. Of modest intelligence (I have "inferior endowments from nature" he said of himself), Washington was a skilled mediator who could command the loyalty or respect of such unlikes as Thomas Jefferson and Alexander Hamilton. And when his powers of persuasion failed, he had a formidable temper that made men quake in their buckled shoes. In Europe he was called "Cincinnatus," for the Roman country gentleman who led an army to save the empire, then refused all honors and the dictator's crown.

But beyond a man there needed to be a spirit. Precedents that we take for granted today as "American" had yet to be set: "As the first of everything *our situation* will serve to establish a precedent," Washington wrote, "it is devoutly wished on my part that these precedents may be fixed on true principles." As a galling symbol of his nation's going-every-which-way difficulties, Washington's new government did not even have a permanent meeting place.

The first capital of the new government was New York City. But, despite the fact that the city had spent much preparing a home for the government, few thought that it would remain the capital. Selection of a final capital was one of "the Rocks which most endangered the safety of the American Union," said one presidential aide. Several states offered sites. They were willing to give up the land, expecting in exchange the prestige and the economic opportunity that most felt certain the capital would bring. From the beginning the government insisted on being master in its own home, without true power being granted to the specially erected non-state.

At the same time, Secretary of the Treasury Alexander Hamilton was addressing himself to "the first symptom of a spirit which must either be killed, or will kill the Constitution." He was facing an attack on the financial responsibility of the federal government itself. Southern states, by and large, had already paid their Revolutionary War debts; thus Secretary of State Jefferson, a Virginian, led the opposition to Hamilton's proposal that the federal government assume such state obligations. Jefferson feared that this display of centralized power would benefit rich northerners most and "Europeanize" the government besides.

ROME AND PARIS, *with their Renaissance and neo-classical plans, gave Washington's early planners visions of vistas and open spaces. The splendor of Paris (opposite) provided the perfect setting for a triumphal parade for Louis XVIII. The grandeur of St. Peter's in Rome (right) offered the double idea of an obelisk and a tall dome.*

It is hard to imagine two more different men than the rangy Virginian and the small, neat New Yorker. Like many of the "founding fathers" they considered each other brothers only in the name of American liberty, while fiercely disagreeing about how to perpetuate it. Jefferson, a believer in "noble Yeomen" and the virtue of agrarian society, had penned the immortal idea "all men are created equal." Hamilton, who suggested modeling the presidency on the English monarchy, feared too much power in the hands of the people. "Your people, sir, is a great beast," he said to those expounding on the virtues of democracy.

Because of the contrasting roles they played in bringing our capital of contrasts into being, the two men are worth examining in depth. Architect, inventor, scientist, farmer as well as statesman and political philosopher, Jefferson was an inspired amateur, a man who did many things for the love of them. He was the embodiment of an Enlightenment ideal: the universal man and a genius of many parts. A slave owner, he later espoused emancipation and freed his chattels upon his death. Born a Virginia aristocrat, he nonetheless scorned formality and fancy dress. A tall man with a "loose and shackling air," he was called "the diplomat in bedroom slippers." In sharp contrast, Hamilton was intense, interested mainly in law and partrician political theory, and driven by sternly disciplined intellect. He was born in the West Indies with an ax to grind: though the grandson of a French Huguenot physician and a Scottish laird, his birth was illegitimate, an accident that honed his ambition. "My blood is as good as that of those who plume themselves on their ancestry" he said, and he married into one of New York's oldest aristocratic families. Orphaned as a boy, Hamilton worked as a ship clerk for a merchant who brought him to New York, his adopted city where he made influential friends. By the eve of the Revolution he had finagled a commission in the colonial militia, then began to write anti-British pamphlets. Within a year he became an aide to

General Washington, who lacked a son as sorely as the 21-year-old artillery officer missed a father. Given to silk stockings, damask waistcoats, frilled shirts, powdered wigs and ordered thoughts, Hamilton was probably infuriated by Jefferson's habit of glancing about, looking at everything but the person he was talking to.

Dissonant as they were, both were committed to the survival of the new nation. Bargaining over supper in New York, Jefferson agreed to lend his considerable influence in the South to federal assumption of the state debts. In return, Hamilton would persuade his fellow northerners to support the principle of a southern capital. Fittingly, the most political of all cities owed its birth to a political compromise.

The Compromise of 1790 stipulated that for the next ten years Congress would meet in Philadelphia, the largest and most cosmopolitan American city. Meanwhile, a 10-mile square would be selected and ceded to the federal government by the states within whose borders it lay. The site was to be on the Potomac River, along the Maryland-Virginia boundary, somewhere between the Anacostia River and Conococheague Creek (100 miles upstream near the village of Williamsport, Maryland). A three-man commission was to select the specific location, but President Washington took personal charge.

He was familiar with the area, having surveyed much of it as a young man and having served as president of the Potomac Company which sought to improve navigation on the river. He toured potential sites possibly with an eye to good public relations, and was cheered "with demonstrations of joy." Some in government insisted that the new capital be built above the port of Georgetown and above the Potomac's first falls, making it inaccessible to a seaborne enemy in time of war. But it seems Washington always believed the city should straddle the river at a navigable point so that a commercial port could develop.

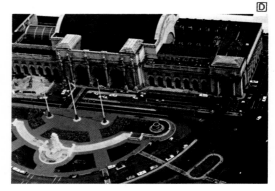

TRAVELING TO THE CAPITAL *today, many of the 20 million annual visitors arrive via National Airport (above, left) or Union Station (above).*

MOVING TO WASHINGTON *in 1800 was a headache for government officials used to the urban elegance of Philadelphia (below) and ill prepared for the riverside rigors of the frontier site between Maryland and Virginia. The cartoon at right ridicules Philadelphia financier Robert Morris' reasons for wanting the capital in his home town.*

"We hear that the President of the United States has ordered three plats of different parts of the Potomac be laid out," a Maryland newspaper whispered. In fact Washington and two fellow Virginians, Jefferson and James Madison, probably considered only one site seriously. They all wanted the capital to include Alexandria which was "beyond all comparison the handsomest town in all Virginia," according to one French visitor. But it lay south on the area describing in the Compromise and defined in the Residence Act.

On January 22, 1791, Washington named the three commissioners who were to select the site for the city and then, presumably, oversee its development. Two days later the President shocked Congress by announcing that he had chosen a spot

and wanted to amend the legislative guidelines to include it. "I am really surprised at the Conduct of the President" one Senator complained. Another archly observed the personal stake Washington had in "Alexandria, contiguous to which is his estate," Mount Vernon. After grumbling, Congress amended the Residence Act.

With the general location established, Washington again preempted the commissioners and appointed a surveyor to delineate the 10-mile square. He chose Andrew Ellicott, scion of the Maryland family who had founded Ellicott City and possessor of the best surveying and celestial sighting equipment on this continent. His remarkable assistant was a self-educated black farmer, Benjamin Banneker, whose exceptional talents may

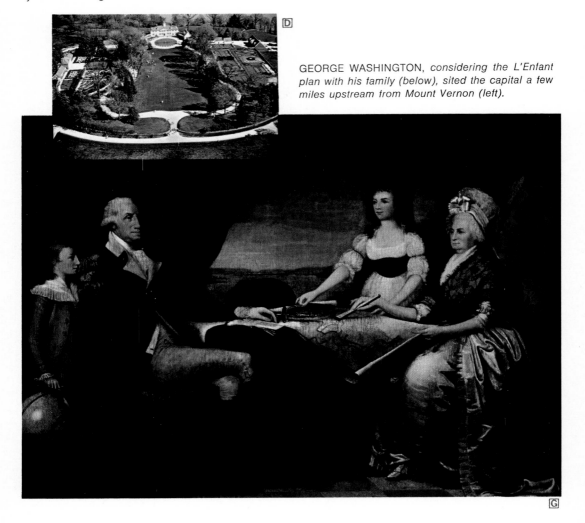

GEORGE WASHINGTON, *considering the L'Enfant plan with his family (below), sited the capital a few miles upstream from Mount Vernon (left).*

have been instrumental in changing one celebrated southerner's mind about racial inferiority. A local paper described Banneker as "an Ethiopian whose abilities as a surveyor and astronomer clearly prove that Mr. Jefferson's concluding that race of men were void of mental endowments was without foundation."

The square they surveyed had sides 10 miles long and corners closely aligned to the cardinal points of the compass. The 77th meridian of longitude passed through the square slightly east of the north and south corners and some Yankee geographers hoped this line would replace the Greenwich meridian as the alpha-omega point for global navigators.

While Ellicott and Banneker were taking their sights, Washington named a chief engineer for the city: Pierre L'Enfant, artist, adventurer and spectacularly arrogant visionary. Trained at the Paris Royal Academy by his father, who had painted murals at Versailles, the young man had followed General Lafayette to the Revolution in 1776. Commissioned a lieutenant, he distinguished himself as an engineer before being captured in Charleston, S.C., and was imprisoned until exchanged for a Hessian in 1782. A man of many talents, he redesigned the New York City Hall, where Washington was inaugurated, for Congressional use. He also designed insignia for the Society of the Cincinnati. (The genealogical organization maintains patrician headquarters in a stately mansion at the foot of Embassy Row on Massachusetts Avenue, N.W. just below Sheridan Circle.)

PIERRE L'ENFANT, *prime architect of the capital, is portrayed at right, superimposed upon his first scheme for Washington.*

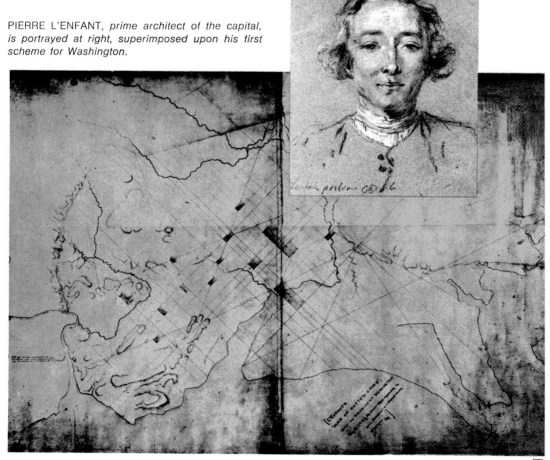

L'Enfant's assignment was less that of an engineer than of a city planner. With Washington's consent, Jefferson ordered him to determine the "grounds most likely . . . for the site of the Federal town and buildings." Arriving in Georgetown in March, 1791, L'Enfant or "Longfont" as Washington mistakenly called him, brought such enthusiasm to his job that even a cold drizzle could not dampen his spirits. No area "in America can be more susceptible to grand improvement than that between the eastern branch of the Potomac [the Anacostia River] and Georgetown," he claimed, and his artist's eye saw Jenkins Hill — the present Capitol Hill, — as "a pedestal awaiting a monument." The partial plan he showed Washington in August was drawn "on such a scale as to leave room for that aggrandisement and embellishment which the increase of the wealth of the Nation will permit it to pursue at any period however remote."

Avenues 160 feet wide would radiate from verdant circles crowned with heroic sculpture. Determined to avoid "tiresome and insipid" vistas, the designer planned a grid of lesser streets whose repetition was broken by the broad boulevards. Along his Mall, which was to be landscaped like the formal gardens of Europe, he called for a canal running to the foot of Capitol Hill. The Capitol building itself would be one of the city's focal points. The city's principal ceremonial street, Pennsylvania Avenue, would run arrow-straight from Congress' home to the President's House, the other focal point. While borrowing ideas from Versailles, Rome and London, the grand plan was an original combination of parts.

"The work of Major L'Enfant . . . is greatly admired," wrote Washington. But his temperament was not. To raise money for construction, the commissioners planned the sale of alternate city lots at public

COMMERCIAL DEVELOPMENT *of Washington by means of its ports (below) remained an elusive dream.*

auction. L'Enfant flatly refused to release his map of the city for early printing, because that would invite speculation.

Daniel Carroll was one of the city's wealthiest men but just as much in the dark about the plan's specifics as everybody else. When he began building a house in the path of New Jersey Avenue, L'Enfant ordered an assistant to tear it down. After the aide was arrested, L'Enfant set out to raze the building himself. The President rebuked him: ''I must strictly enjoin you to touch no man's property without his consent.'' But much as L'Enfant revered Washington, he loved the city — his creation — more. His obstinancy grew worse until the following March when Jefferson wrote: ''I am instructed by the President to inform you that notwithstanding the desire he has entertained to preserve your agency in the business, the condition upon which it is to be done is inadmissable & your services must be at an end.''

L'Enfant went north, laid out Paterson, N.J., but returned to the capital to demand $95,000 for his services from Congress (which ultimately gave him $3800). Apparently he did little work thereafter; he became a ''character'' wandering around the city, haranging anyone who would listen and living off the charity of friends, dying a pauper in 1825. Nearly a century later his remains were ceremoniously reburied at Arlington National Cemetery.

Though he was on the job less than a year, Pierre L'Enfant directed the city's growth. He conceived the seminal plan of the capital and the modern city bears the stamp of his designing hand.

Surveyor Ellicott, a man of ''more placid temper,'' was assigned to finish L'Enfant's map which he did, altering it slightly, deleting the original designer's name and adding his own. The ''Ellicott Map'' was distributed widely in hopes of encouraging public responses to a second auction. This also failed to raise much money.

(continued on page 46)

REAL ESTATE DEVELOPMENT *of Washington's rolling terrain was an economic and engineering challenge.*

BENJAMIN BANNEKER, *surveyor of the capital, was also known to his contemporaries as the purveyor of scientific information by means of his* Almanac, *which is superimposed below upon a letter from Jefferson (left) advancing his cause to scientific societies in Europe.*

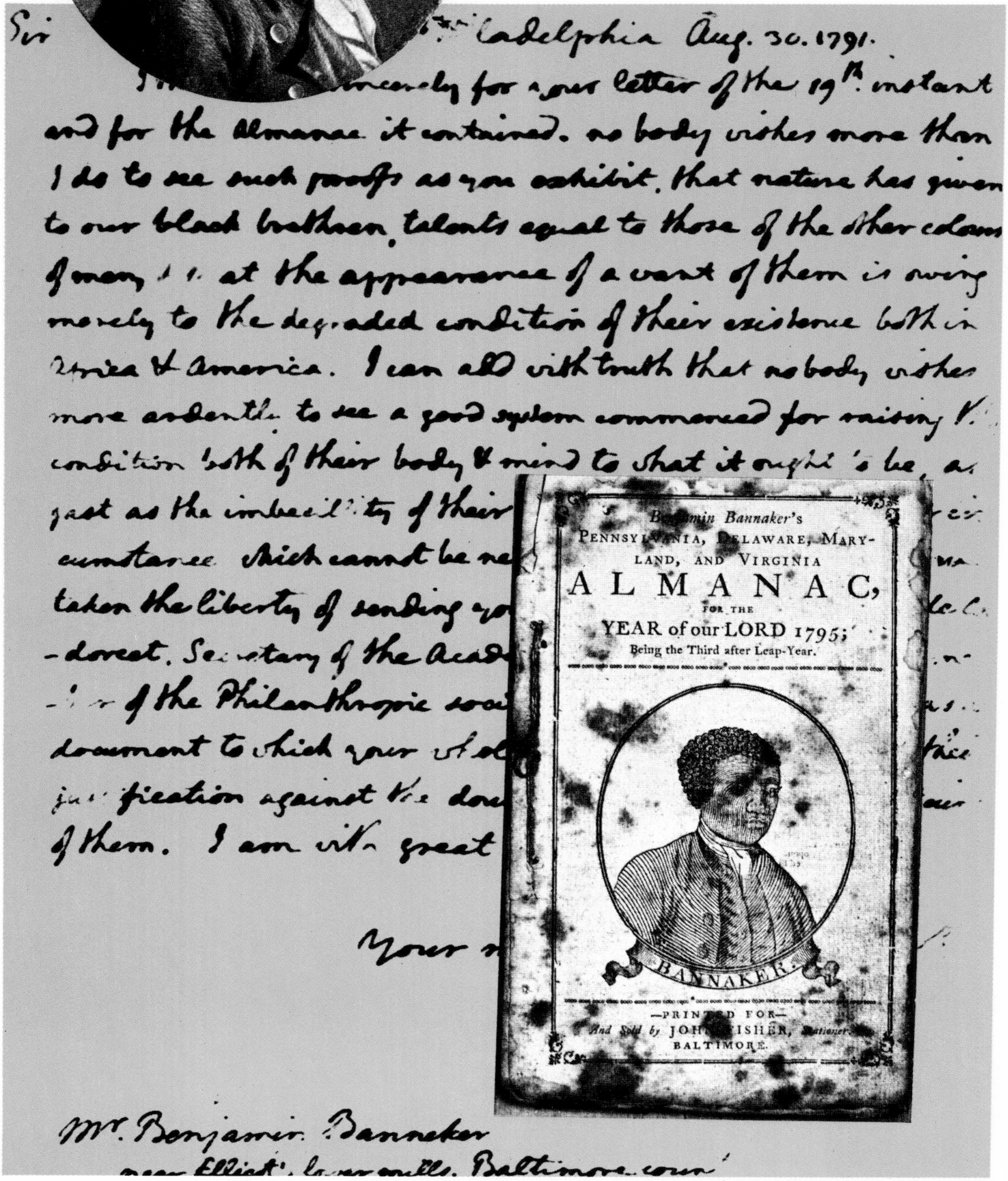

Sir   ...iladelphia Aug. 30. 1791.

I ... sincerely for your letter of the 19th instant and for the Almanac it contained. no body wishes more than I do to see such proofs as you exhibit, that nature has given to our black brethren, talents equal to those of the other colours of men & & at the appearance of a want of them is owing merely to the degraded condition of their existence both in Africa & America. I can add with truth that no body wishes more ardently to see a good system commenced for raising the condition both of their body & mind to what it ought to be, as fast as the imbecility of their ... present existence ... circumstance which cannot be ne... ... taken the liberty of sending your ... ...docet. Secretary of the Acad... ...r of the Philanthropic soci... ...document to which your wh... ...justification against the dou... ...of them. I am with great ...

Your m...

Benjamin Bannaker's
PENNSYLVANIA, DELAWARE, MARY-
LAND, AND VIRGINIA
ALMANAC,
FOR THE
YEAR of our LORD 1795;
Being the Third after Leap-Year.

BANNAKER.

—PRINTED FOR—
And Sold by JOHN FISHER, Stationer,
BALTIMORE.

Mr. Benjamin Banneker
near Elliot's lower mills, Baltimore coun'

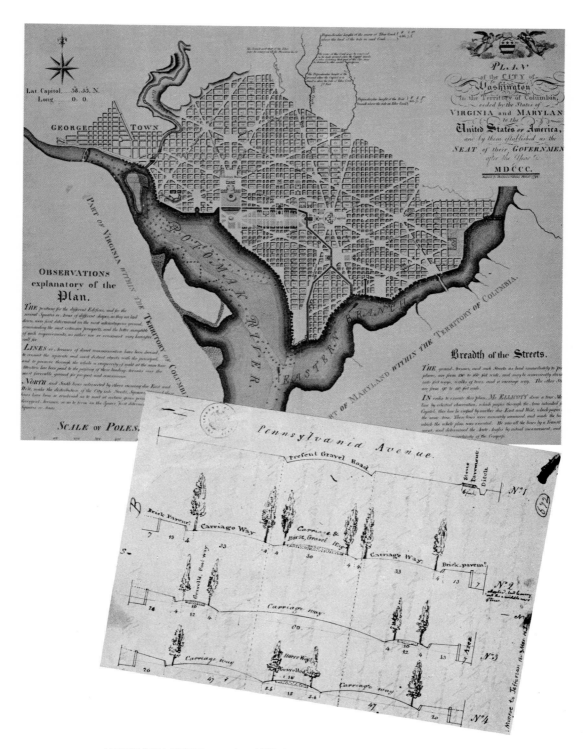

ANDREW ELLICOTT *completed L'Enfant's design. With his plan above is Jefferson's sketch for a poplar shaded Pennsylvania Avenue.*

(continued from page 43)

Hoping to fulfill Washington's wish to have a "habitable city by 1800," the commissioners announced design competitions for the Capitol and the President's House. Theirs was a brave gambit, because the nation had few trained architects and no indigenous style for public buildings. It was not surprising then that the designs submitted borrowed heavily on a wide variety of European models — as indeed the ideas behind the Declaration and Constitution owed a similar debt to French and English thinkers. Washington had expressed the wish that the city's major buildings be edifices of "size, form and elegance."

The competition for the President's House went well. Almost to a man, the designers offered size, at least. One highly sophisticated drawing was signed only "A.Z." Thomas Jefferson's interest ran from architecture to zoology. But the plan submitted by an Irish builder named James Hoban won the competition. It conformed to Washington's ideas and followed L'Enfant's desire to combine "the sumptuousness of a palace and the agreeableness of a country seat."

The Capitol competition brought slow results. The design of Etienne Hallet; a young French-born architect, was promising but unacceptable. Hallet was told to rework his design. Then a Philadelphia physician and amateur architect (who received word of the competition belatedly) requested and received permission to offer a design after the deadline. When William Thornton's plan arrived, it was quickly approved. In Jefferson's words: "It is simple, noble, beautiful, excellently arranged and moderate in size." Thornton's design called for a low-domed rotunda with a short wing on each side — essentially the inner sections of the present building.

(continued on page 52)

A LOW-PROFILE CAPITOL *was proposed by winning architect William Thornton in his original presentation. The painting of his edifice below shows it as it appeared about 1840, with dome designed by Charles Bullfinch.*

GRAND AND PECULIAR *ideas helped the Capitol's development—from the statue-studded
facade below to the chamber plans by
Latrobe (right).*

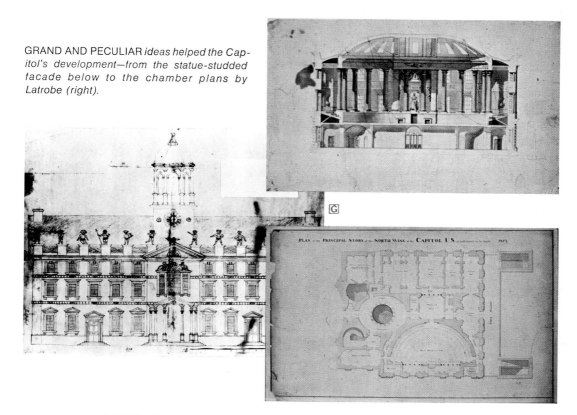

G

A HIGH-RISE CAPITOL *soars above other federal buildings below. By law, no
structure in the city may be loftier.*

D

Master Builders of Early Washington

Like few other American cities, Washington has a special, splendid look because of a number of great architects.

William Thornton, the prize-winning architect of the Capitol, also designed the famed Octagon House and beautiful Tudor Place at 1544 31st Street in Georgetown. Thornton, a trained physician whose hobby was architecture, made his name and a fortune as a designer. James Hoban, the designer of the White House, based his plan on the home of the Duke of Leicester in Dublin, Ireland. Like many of our nation's early architects, the Irish-born Hoban brought schooling and techniques learned from abroad to his plans. Hoban also designed Blodgett's "Great Hotel," which served as home for Congress after the war of 1812.

Washington was, for many years, the base of Benjamin H. Latrobe, the "father of American architecture." English by birth and training, Latrobe left a distinctive impression on Washington; his St. John's Church and Decatur House on Lafayette Square established the pattern for that area, and subsequent work on the White House and Capitol showed the effect of his subtle genius. A friend of Jefferson, Latrobe died penniless in New Orleans in 1820.

Another English architect (and like Latrobe, another follower of the Greek Revival Style) was George Hadfield. Hadfield, who often sided with Latrobe in the latter's frequent battles with Thornton, is remembered by the City Hall, now the D.C. Court House on 4th and D Streets, N.W., and Arlington House, The Robert E. Lee Memorial (the official name, recently adopted) overlooking Arlington Cemetery. More fortunate than Latrobe, Hadfield lived well in his later days.

Remaining in the Greek Revival tradition of Latrobe and Hadfield was Robert Mills. Probably the first native American to be trained in the architect's profession, Mills studied under Hoban and Latrobe. The Latrobe influence can be seen in Mills' work on the Treasury Building, the old Post Office on F Street, N.W. (now the Tariff Commission) and the Washington Monument.

The pervasive influence of the Greek Revival school of architecture was broken by James Renwick. His design for the Smithsonian Castle was acclaimed for its utilitarian usage of space. So impressed was one particular Washingtonian, William W. Corcoran, that Renwick became more or less his resident architect, designing the Corcoran Art Gallery (now the Renwick), Corcoran's own house, and a chapel for Corcoran in the Oak Hill Cemetery in Georgetown. As the Civil War approached, the more utilitarian style of architecture became popular. The works of Adolf Cluss, a refugee from the German Revolution of 1848, can be seen in the Eastern Market and the Franklin School on 13th Street, N.W. For the most part, however, that part of pre-Civil War Washington that can still be seen is boldly Greek Revival in style.

ARCHITECTURAL GENIUS *of William Thornton stands forth from the porticoed facade of Tudor Place (shown with the architect's portrait opposite) as well as from the Capitol. Elegant brick Tudor Place is still in the ownership of a descendant of the Washingtons.*

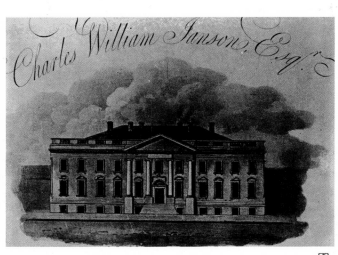

JAMES HOBAN'S CONCEPT *of the Presidential Mansion was carefully fulfilled in its construction as attested by the contemporary sketch in traveller Charles Janson's book (right). The building's shape and facade were not dissimilar to the architect's Blodgett's Hotel (above in 1803 painting).*

A PALLADIAN DESIGN *for the White House (right) was submitted by "A. Z." who turned out to be Thomas Jefferson —man of the ever-ready pen.*

SPRING BRIGHT, *the White House appears across Pennsylvania Avenue from Lafayette Square.*

FROM THE ELLIPSE *behind the White House sightseers may glimpse acres of lawn—and possibly a Presidential event.*

(continued from page 46)

Since Etienne Hallet was a practiced architect and Thornton was not, the former was appointed to supervise construction; by the spring of 1793 work was underway. Arguing that the original design was too difficult to build, Hallet made it easier by introducing many of his own ideas. This irked Thronton and a power struggle ensued — ending with Hallet's dismissal and Thornton's promotion to the commission. Meanwhile, lack of construction money from the misbegotten land auctions slowed the construction pace and contributed to labor problems. Recruited for the work, many "mechanicks and labourers from Europe" found on arrival that "a great portion of the labor . . . now in progress . . . is performed by slaves" leased from nearby plantations. Hopes that bloomed with the ceremonial laying of the cornerstone on September 18, 1793, quickly faded.

Strapped for funds, the commissioners were unfortunately willing to endorse almost any money-making scheme. Samuel Blodgett, an agressive land dealer, had wrangled a job as superintendent in charge of public buildings. He suggested a lottery, the first prize being "a superb hotel with bath, outhouses, etc. etc." worth $50,000 and designed by James Hoban, already famous for his presidential mansion. If the scheme made sense in the beginning, it failed to net many dollars in the end: Blodgett ran one lottery and, when it failed even to pay for itself, ran another which was also a failure. Matters became more confused and building schedules further delayed. Washington passed on to Jefferson the tales of woe he was hearing from the commissioners: "Little confidence, I fear, is placed in Mr. Blodgett, and least where he is best known." Blodgett soon

(continued on page 56)

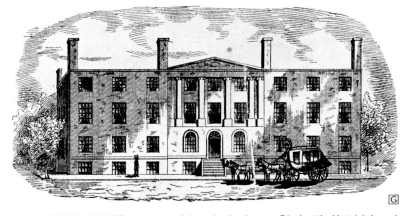

THE PATENT OFFICE *took up lodgings in the former Blodgett's Hotel (above). There ingenious Americans registered such inventions as the artist's tool and the shower below.*

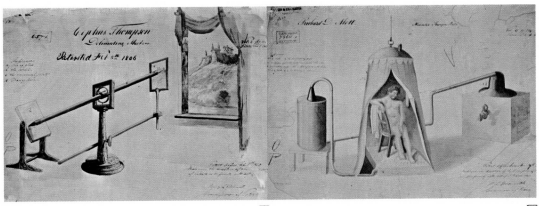

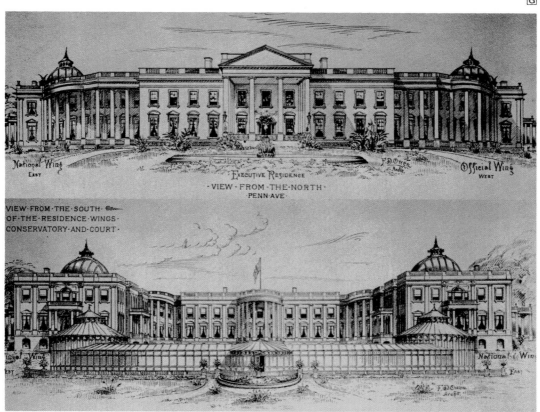

CHANGING IDEAS *for the White House, not all of which have been well considered or actually carried out, have kept the mansion in a state of flux. The grandiose scheme above, embracing a green house, was advanced by Mrs. Benjamin Harrison. Dolley Madison's White House appears below.*

The Many Mansions of The Executive Branch

The Judicial branch of the government occupies the Supreme Court Building, and the Legislative is housed by the Capitol and the House and Senate Office Buildings. But the Executive, the third co-equal branch of government, occupies innumerable buildings throughout the city and suburbs.

The White House and the neighboring Executive Office Building are the nerve center of the branch. The Treasury Building, the oldest departmental building, thrusts its bulk out onto Pennsylvania Avenue just east of the White House.

Further east is Washington's largest government enclave, the Federal Triangle. The Commerce Department Building takes up the entire block between 14th and 15th Streets, N.W. Designed by York and Sawyer Associates, it includes an interesting aquarium in its basement. Neighboring the Commerce Department Building on Constitution Avenue — the other border of the Federal Triangle besides Pennsylvania Avenue and 14th Street — are the Labor Department and the Interstate Commerce Commission, both designed by Arthur Brown and completed in 1935. The Post Office Department, designed by Delano and Aldrich Associates, and the Justice Department, by Zartzinger, Bon and Meday Associates, stand next to one another on the south side of Pennsylvania Avenue.

Across 9th Street from the Justice Department is the National Archives Building. John R. Pope designed this handsome structure which exhibits those vital founding documents of the United States Government — the Declaration of Independence and the Constitution. To the east of the Archives Building is the Bennett, Parson and Frost designed Federal Trade Commission Building marked by massive granite statuary. Across Pennsylvania Avenue stands the most recent addition to the Triangle, the F.B.I. Building, named in honor of its first director, J. Edgar Hoover. Tours of this building, which was designed by C.F. Murphy Associates, give many visitors an especially vivid memory of their trip to Washington.

Some more recently organized executive agencies are located across the Mall from the Federal Triangle. Much of the Health, Education and Welfare Department is housed in the building on the corner of Independence Avenue and 4th Street, S.W. which features a lobby mural by Ben Shahn. West of the H.E.W. Building along Independence Avenue stand the headquarters of two other executive departments. The Housing and Urban Development Department is housed in a swooping structure designed by Marcel Breuer, and the Transportation Department in an elegant pavillion by Edward Durrell Stone. Farther west along Independence Avenue are the Agriculture Department's two buildings, which are connected by an interesting arch over Independence Avenue. And just across 14th Street from the Agriculture Department is the massive Bureau of Engraving and Printing designed by James G. Hill; here all the paper money in America is printed. Tours of this building are always tempting.

With the State Department in Foggy Bottom, the massive Pentagon (home of the Defense Department) near Arlington, the Central Intelligence Agency in McLean, Virginia and other agencies scattered throughout the area, the size of the Executive branch demonstrates the dynamic outreach of our government.

CLASSICAL AND MODERN *architecture serve Washington's federal establishment. The Archives Building (above), and the Treasury Building (right) stand in stark contrast to the government structures of Washington's new Southwest.*

(continued from page 52)

moved on, but his memory lingered in the form of an unfinished hotel and a series of lawsuits brought by the Philadelphian who bought the winning $8 ticket.

With the auction failing and Blodgett's scheme a laughingstock, the city grew slowly and irregularly. The few houses built were clustered at one or the other end of Pennsylvania Avenue with most of the center section remaining little more than a bog. L'Enfant had feared this and in fact had planned that "the main establishment . . . should be . . . equidistant as possible from the center." His plan to bring activity to the central portion of the Federal establishment by placing the judiciary there, north of Pennsylvania Avenue and half-way between the White House and Capitol, never materialized. Instead, this co-equal branch of government was left, more or less, to fend for itself. From 1801 until 1935 the Supreme Court met in the Capitol and, when the room there was unavailable, in private homes. The Court's room in the Capitol was so tucked away, that a visitor from New York wrote, "one might traverse the dark avenues of the Capitol for a week without finding the remote corner in which justice is administered to the American Republic." Despite their inauspicious surroundings, the Justices took occasional time out for fun. John Marshall and his companions liked a bit of wine to liven spirits on rainy days, and in fact Marshall might ask a Justice to "step to the window to see if it doesn't look like rain." When the answer was no, Marshall would often request the wine anyway, saying: "Our jurisdiction is so vast that it must be raining somewhere."

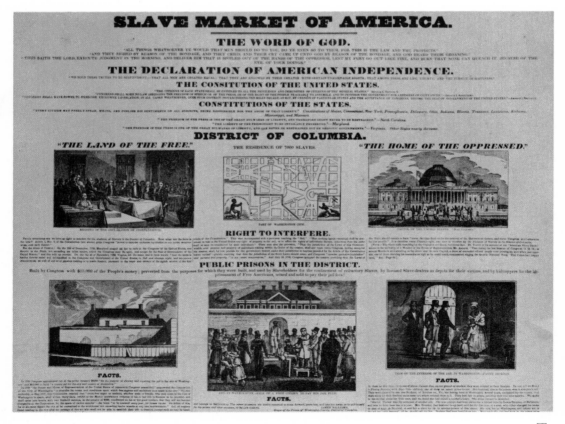

TRAFFIC IN SLAVES, *long a fact of life in Washington, was the cause of many protests. The broadside above proclaims the immorality of slavery.*

The Federal City's growth was agonizingly slow, and the man for whom it was named died before its development was certain. His successor, President John Adams prodded Congress past the point of no return in May 1800, shortly after Washington's death. It was then resolved that on the third Monday in November of that year, Congress would convene in the new Capitol willy-nilly. The district may still have been a ''howling, malarial wilderness'' but Adams ordered executive department heads to take steps that ''public offices may be opened in the city of Washington for the dispatch of business by the 15th of June.'' The first to arrive in late May, was the Post Office, which set up shop in an unfinished row house.

While the other departments were preparing for their move, President Adams set out for his own inspection of the city. After a triumphal tour that stopped in many towns along the way, he arrived in a spring-bright city that looked beautiful, at first glance, despite the unpaved streets. ''The public buildings,'' at least, were ''in a much greater forwardness'' than expected, he wrote (though his wife complained about lack of firewood and, moving into the President's House, had the laundry hung to dry in the East Room). Treasury Secretary Oliver Wolcott was unenthusiastic: ''There are few houses in any one place, and most of them [are] small miserable huts. . . . I do not perceive how the members of Congress can possibly secure lodgings unless they will consent to live like scholars in a college or monks in a monastary.''

G

DEDICATED TO FREEDOM, *the United States depended heavily upon slave labor to construct the public buildings in the capital. The slaves (right) return from work on the Capitol, while below slaves are brought ashore into bondage.*

UNITED STATES SLAVE TRADE.
1850.

G

In fact, most Congressmen hesitated to bring their families to this rawboned outpost but, instead, lived in boarding houses when the legislature was in session. These hostels soon had the earmarks of college fraternities; a man could be politically identified by his lodgings. Legislative plans were laid at dinner in the "congressional messes." One Congressman was ostracized for taking a political stand contrary to his boardinghouse mates.

Senator Gouverneur Morris, a caustic Pennsylvanian, sneered: "We want nothing here but houses, [wine] cellars, kitchens, well-informed men, amiable women, and other trifles of this kind to make our city perfect." An English visitor wrote, about this time, that the city "will not come to perfection for . . . two centuries if it ever does at all." Others saw Washington as a "city in ruins" and found their situation "both melancholy and ludicrous."

But it was, at least, a place where things were starting to happen, a city with its own style, wit and purpose: politics, which eclipsed almost everything else, especially in those years when the men of government were powerfully aware of creating precedents almost every time they turned around.

When Jefferson succeeded Adams, in 1801, the one-time political allies had long since split in bitterness. Adams didn't even stay to attend Jefferson's inauguration. The Virginian brought a lively informality to the capital scene—and appalled foreign ambassadors with the absence of conventional manners. But apparently the cuisine was impressive and the drink vintage: Jefferson's wine bill was $2000 one year; he spent $7000 more than his salary of $25,000 (and, like his old enemy Hamilton, died on the verge of poverty, having sold his books to the Library of Congress). Adams and Jefferson became close friends again through fertile correspondence about the problems of the struggling nation that had more than doubled its size with Jefferson's Louisiana Purchase. The accidents of death among Washington personalities were curious in this period. On the fiftieth anniversary of the Declaration of Independence, Adams lay on his death bed in Quincy, Massachusetts. His last words were: "thank God, Jefferson still lives." But the Virginian had died that morning, July 4, 1826, at Monticello.

The men who brought it into existence no longer walked the capital's muddy streets. The air of pomp and ceremony that Washington had wanted was lacking. But the Capitol was there. While it and the surrounding city were hardly fitting symbols of ideal democracy, the place had survived infancy as a city "which so many [were] willing to come to and all [were] anxious to leave."

FROM HUMBLE BEGINNINGS *the Capitol has grown to soaring magnificence (opposite, top). The East Front, as it appeared from 1824-1856, is depicted opposite, below. Though less awesome than the 1863 Walter Dome, the Capitol's old Bulfinch Dome, (below) dominated the Washington skyline in the mid-1800's.*

G

The Embattled Capital

In 1810, twenty years after its founding, Washington remained more of a mud-tracked village than a city. Of its 24,000 inhabitants, one-quarter were slaves and half lived in the older towns of Alexandria and Georgetown. Congressmen called it a "Golgatha of numbskulls" and a "hateful place." It was "an abode of splendid misery," topped off by an incomplete Capitol, with a crude covered bridge connecting the North and South Wings. The building would lack its imposing center portion for another fourteen years.

Still, the Congress could be counted on to put its own houses in order — and to neglect the surrounding city whose purse strings it held in a miserly fist. In the first eighty years, the House of Representatives would spend more money on the Capitol alone than on the entire capital city. More money was appropriated annually for the President's salary than for municipal projects. Such things as street improvements were funded by local taxes, though a major portion of the city's assets were federally owned and therefore tax exempt. (This fiscal nicety was confirmed by the Supreme Court in the landmark decision,

INTO THE HEARTLAND *the Potomac opens a broad pathway, as seen in this 1850 view of Washington from above Georgetown.*

G

McCulloch v. Maryland, in 1819; today the federal government contributes about one-quarter of the city's operating budget).

Thus, Washington's and Jefferson's dream of a beautiful capital city belonging to all the people — because all the people paid for it — seemed beyond reach. The burden of making the place liveable fell on a handful of residents who could hardly afford the price. Then in 1814 the barely attainable dream was nearly lost forever among the battle smoke of what some historians call "the Second War of Independence."

Primarily a naval conflict, the War of 1812 would confirm America's right to western lands and free trade with continental Europe. But before its conclusion, the British attacked Washington in an attempt to demoralize the new nation into surrender and in retribution for the firing of York, Canada. A British force sailed up the Patuxent River in July 1814, and marched overland to Bladensburg where defenders of the capital's outposts were routed in half-an-hour.

On the evening of August 24 the redcoats camped on the flat high ground east of the Capitol. Nearly all officials had fled. Dolley Madison left in a carriage with the executive mansion's silver service and the famous Gilbert Stuart portrait of George Washington. The few Yankee soldiers who stayed in the territory retired to the Navy Yard (which still stands on the Anacostia). There they burned a ship on the ways along with most portable supplies, lest these fall into enemy hands, and dispersed.

Under foppish Rear Admiral George Cockburn, an undistinguished aristocrat whose career peaked with this raid, the British burned Washington. They put almost every public building to the torch but observed a certain martial chivalry: little private property was destroyed and civilians were pointedly not molested. The only official structure to escape the fire was saved by a combination of audacious American courage and Georgian respect for invention. It was the Patent Office (Blodgett's Hotel slightly renovated). As the British trained artillery on the building, William Thornton threw himself over the muzzle of the cannon crying: "Are you Englishmen or Goths and Vandals?" Published accounts of what he said next strain modern imagin-

OPEN TO THE ENEMY, *the riverside capital was struck from both land and sea in the War of 1812.*

ation, given the extremity of the situation and his awkward posture. ''This is the Patent Office,'' he supposedly proclaimed, ''the repository of the inventive genius of America, in which the whole civilized world is concerned. Would you destroy it? If so, fire away and let the charge pass through my body.''

But he could only block one gun and British torches were everywhere. The Treasury and Post Office burned. The President's House was gutted. The Capitol was virtually destroyed after troops used its furniture and library's infant collection for tinder. The destruction would have been complete but for furious rain and gales. The storm caused some of the few casualties among the invaders, while others were injured by an accidental explosion of a gunpowder cache discovered in a Navy Yard well. One redcoat, hurled high through the air by the blast to land safely in a tree, chose to remain in the United States and dined off his bizarre experience for years.

Concerned for his fleet in the tempest that tore roofs away and quenched the flames, Admiral Cockburn ordered a withdrawal. Outside his headquarters on the corner of F and 15th Streets, N.W. (a tavern then, an eclectic ''newsstand'' now), he met a feisty young woman. ''Great God, madam,'' the admiral declaimed, ''Is this the kind of storm of which you are accustomed in this infernal country?'' She answered, ''No sir. This is a special interposition of Providence to drive our enemies from our city.''

Much of England was shocked by the arson. ''The Cossacks spared Paris,'' wrote the London Statesman, ''but we spared not the Capital of America.'' Still, their shame did not compare with the emotions of Potomac region residents whose spirit was nearly broken. However slow their progress had been, it now seemed their city was doomed. When Congress met, it debated moving the seat of government elsewhere, the House defeated the resolution by a slim nine votes. Senate support had to be marshalled by local bankers who volunteered to give low interest loans for the restoration of public buildings.

"In the Hall of Representatives the devastation has been dreadful," wrote Benjamin H. Latrobe, the architect charged with the repairs. President Madison returned to find his official residence barely standing. Months later he signed the war-resolving Treaty of Ghent in the Octagon House, one of his temporary homes and now the charming adjunct of the American Institute of Architect's headquarters at 18th Street and New York Avenue, N.W. Three years after the fire President Monroe moved back into the restored mansion. Its smoke-stained sandstone walls had been painted, lending a new look and assuring it the name it has carried ever since: White House.

Meanwhile, Congress had been homeless too. At first it occupied the single undamaged public building. But the Patent Office became so cramped that legislators perched "in every spot up to the fireplace and the windows." While the resourceful Latrobe worked to restore the Capitol, private citizens formed a company that hastily built a meeting place. The temporary "Brick Capitol," ugly as it was, worked effectively. It moved a poet to rhapsodize:

"And the new edifice in splendor Sprung/ Like a Phoenix from its ashes." Before being razed from the spot now occupied by the Supreme Court, this unsplendid "tempo" served as legislative hall, jail, and warehouse. The citizens had met the challenge.

With the fear of the government's departure removed, Washingtonians began to improve the city. The most fashionable neighborhood to develop in this period faced the White House across Pennsylvania Avenue. Benjamin Latrobe marked the square's northern boundary in 1816 with the completion of St. John's Church — "the Church of Presidents" as it is now-called. Then he designed Stephen Decatur's house, which remains today on Jackson Place across from the square's northwest corner, now, fittingly, a naval museum operated by the National Trust for Historic Preservation. In 1825 the square was named Lafayette Park for the Revolution's French hero who, returning on a sentimental visit called the city "the central star of the constellation which enlightens the world."

(continued on page 67)

ARSONIST OF WASHINGTON, *Admiral George Cockburn stands before the blazing city in the portrait at right. British troops under General Robert Ross had come overland from the Patuxent River and had defeated the American Militia at Blandensburg (above) before striking at the capital.*

"MR. MADISON'S WAR," *as the bitter conflict of 1812 was called, brought humiliation to that statesman-like President. In the cartoon opposite, two British sailors mock him as he flees from the burning capital while in the background bemused citizens taunt him with political slogans.*

DOLLEY MADISON, *portrayed opposite by Gilbert Stuart, remains renowned in Washington for her warm hospitality and her cool saving of treasures from the White House before it was set ablaze by the British and pillaged by the citizenry in 1814.*

THE OCTAGON HOUSE, *seen in the fish-eye view at right from the neighboring headquarters of the American Institute of Architects, gave the Madisons a home in post-war Washington. Having in fact six rather than eight sides, the house was designed by William Thornton.*

THE CORNER OF E STREET *(below) was painted by the Baroness de Neuville in the summer of 1817.*

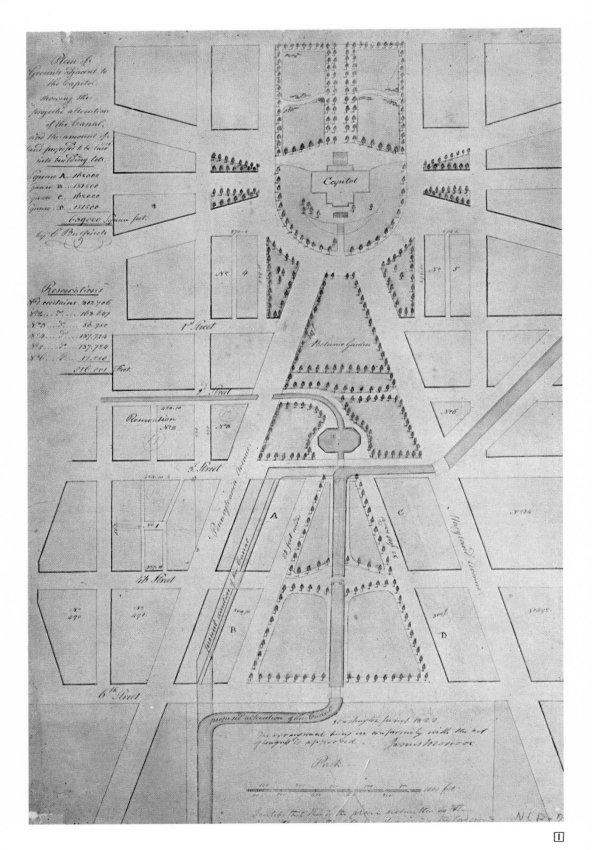

66

(continued from page 63)

During the rest of the century many stately homes rose to face the gardens and heroic statues that enhance what many consider the city's most beautiful park. In our time, the wrecker's ball threatened those harmonious facades to make room for federal offices. Mrs. John F. Kennedy opposed the destruction and inspired a unified plan. It called for mammoth but simple and elegant brick office structures to form a backdrop behind the graceful nineteenth century houses. Restored as offices now, the houses remain to overlook the chess games, secretaries' noontime picnics and occasional rallies that occupy the flowering square. Countless heads of state have been guests on the square in the stucco mansion called the Blair House.

President Harry Truman also lived there from 1948 to 1952 while the White House underwent a major renovation.

Elsewhere in the heart of the city other impressive houses arose. General John P. Van Ness, son-in-law of the obstinant David Burnes who years earlier delayed Pennsylvania Avenue's clearing until his crops ripened, commissioned Latrobe to build a house that was luxurious in the extreme. On the site of today's Pan American Building, it had hot and cold running water in every bedroom. This was indeed an eyebrow-raising accomplishment at a time when many people patronized public bath houses, paying as much as the tax that qualified a resident

G

A CITY OF RURAL LEISURE *was glimpsed by artist August Köllner when he visited the capital in the 1830's. The scene above was painted near Pennsylvania Avenue and 7th Street.*

A CAPITAL OF GARDENS *was envisioned by architect Robert Mills when he presented the plan (opposite) to President Monroe. The Mall would spread out fan-wise between Pennsylvania and Maryland Avenues.*

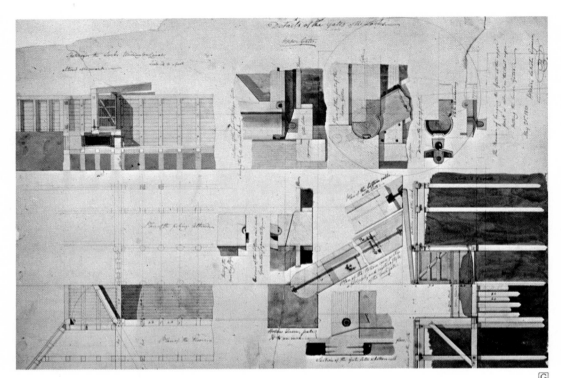

TO WORK A CANAL, *a complex system of gates and levers for the locks had to be devised; the engineering plans above for lock gates were drafted by Benjamin Latrobe.*

TO TAME A RIVER *for purposes of 19th century Washington, the Potomac was bordered by the C & O Canal (foreground, below) and crossed by an aqueduct.*

AQUEDUCT OF POTOMAC, GEORGETOWN D.C.

to vote. One reads that "Saturday and . . . Sunday morning until ten o'clock the price was fifty cents." During the week, baths could be had on an hour's notice but the price was a dollar.

If indoor plumbing was rare, good food was not. Center Market, a collection of sheds and stalls where the Archives Building now stands, midway between Capitol and White House, was famous for produce from nearby farms, fresh-killed game and meat, and delicacies from Chesapeake Bay such as terrapin and oysters. Daniel Webster, known for his discriminating palate as well as his oratory, often vied with housewives when shopping for his cook. The Center Market was commonly known as Marsh Market since the ceremonial avenue of

L'Enfant's plan remained a bog. Drainage was improved somewhat by the opening of the Washington Canal, in 1815, but the problem was not completely solved.

The Canal, which would later link up with the Chesapeake and Ohio Canal, extended from the Potomac (near the present Washington Monument grounds) to the Anacostia River. High hopes that the canal would bring great commercial wealth to the city died quickly as the canal became as much a bog as Tiber Creek which it replaced. Even so, there remained a feeling of high expectations for the city as the so-called "era of good feelings" began. Real estate sales swelled 500 percent, and some Congressmen even bought or built permanent residences in Washington.

TO DELIGHT THE PEOPLE, *the restored C & O Canal (seen below at Great Falls Tavern, now a museum) offers placid stretches for canoeing and fishing.*

Drawn July 1830.

Steamboat Wharf, Washington, D.C.

THE WATERFRONT YESTERDAY *hummed with local activity, both on the wharves (above) and up the Anacostia (below).*

East Branch of Potomac R. Washington.

Fires frequently prodded progress in these decades. The old Patent Office at Blodgett's Hotel burned and was replaced by a building that filled an entire block opposite the then new Post Office on F Street. Its ample halls, built to accommodate such large machines as the reapers for the Midwest's endless grainfields, now display the treasures of the celebrated National Portrait Gallery and Fine Arts Collection. Also along F Street were the homes of some of Washington's most illustrious residents, among them Chief Justice Roger B. Taney. John Quincy Adams, the first ex-president to return to Congress (the only other was Andrew Johnson) lived on the street which now is graced by a lively shopping mall. His sharp-tongued grandson Henry, who later in life moved to the more chic area of Lafayette Square, viewed the new Post Office and Patent Building as "unfinished . . . white Greek Temples in the abandoned gravel pits of a deserted Syrian city."

When the original Treasury burned in 1833, a Jefferson protege named Robert Mills,

was commissioned to design a replacement. Legend has it that President Jackson, tired of Congressional bickering, chose the present site because it would block the White House view of the Capitol. In fact, the new building was built on the footings of the old, probably because a stingy Congress declined to waste the vacant lot, even though it marred L'Enfant's cherished avenue.

In 1835 the city's single theater, a "small and most astonishingly dirty" one, was replaced by the National Theater, which though burned-out several times since still occupies the original site. It boasted boxes "embellished with sketches in bas relief . . . surrounded by . . . ornaments representing brilliant events." For people of other tastes, the Marine Band gave concerts and several gambling houses offered diversion. If that weren't enough for early 19th century tastes, the Baltimore and Ohio Railroad provided transportation to the wide world beyond—although the depot was on the outskirts of town and was reached by horse-drawn shuttles.

(continued on page 74)

THE WATERFRONT TODAY *still bustles: from open-air fish stands on Maine Avenue (below) to the elegance of the promenade along the front of new restaurants in the restored Southwest district (right). Tour boats may take the visitor from the wharves to Mount Vernon; cruise ship lines may take him to the Caribbean.*

Open House At The Smithsonian

The Smithsonian Institution ranks as the chief cultural agency in the city and probably the nation. The main complex of buildings within the Smithsonian stands on the Mall but five major subdivisions are elsewhere.

The Zoological Park on upper Connecticut Avenue was begun in 1889 — from alligators to zebras it contains most species of animals in the world today. Quite a broad cultural jump away is the John F. Kennedy Center for the Performing Arts on Rock Creek Parkway near Virginia Avenue. Designed by Edward D. Stone, the center opened in 1969. Here plays, operas, films and concerts are held throughout the year.

On F Street at 8th, N.W., the renovated Patent Office is the home of the National Portrait Gallery, whose broad variety of portraits lends a personal dimension to United States history. This building also houses the National Collection of Fine Arts, works of many famous and not so famous American artists.

The Renwick Gallery on Pennsylvania Avenue at 17th Street N.W. (the old Corcoran Gallery) offers a particular delight to students of American architecture and crafts. On Martin Luther King Avenue in S.E. Washington, the Smithsonian has a small neighborhood museum which carries various special exhibits in response to area residents.

As important as these elements are, most of the Smithsonian can be visited by walking around the Mall. Today the red sandstone castle, designed by James Renwick in 1855, is primarily used as an administrative headquarters. Directly facing it is the Natural History Museum. Designed by Hornblower and Marshall in 1910, its exhibits focus on man and his surroundings. It includes displays of fossils, specimens of various animals, beautiful gems (including the Hope Diamond) and representations of various forms of human civilizations. Next door, the Museum of History and Technology (the last building designed by the renowned firm of McKim, Meade and White and completed in 1964) features all aspects of American technology and craftsmanship. Printing presses, costumes, steam locomotives, and even the drill rig used to bring oil from Spindletop, Texas in 1901, are exhibited.

Three galleries are also part of the Smithsonian's Mall complex. Just west of the castle the Freer Gallery, designed by Charles A. Platt to house Charles Linz Freer's enormous collection of oriental art, was completed in 1924. In addition to the large collection of Orientalia is a sizeable portion of the works of James McNeil Whistler. Along Independence Avenue beyond the castle is the ornate Arts and Industry Building (designed by Adolf Cluss) now being remodeled as a replica of the Philadelphia Centennial celebration of 1876). The Hirshhorn Museum and Sculpture Garden, designed by Gordon Bunshaft to house Mr. Hirshhorn's excellent collection, was completed in 1974. Across the Mall is the National Gallery of Art. Many of the works here came originally from Andrew Mellon's massive collection of old masters. The building, designed by John Russell Pope, and completed in 1941, is also the scene of concerts both by the National Gallery Orchestra and by soloists, in the East Garden Court. An addition, designed by I.M. Pei is scheduled for 1976 completion.

The newest Smithsonian building is the Air and Space Museum, which will replace the quonset hut that presently houses the collection which includes WW I fighter planes, Charles Lindbergh's "Spirit of St. Louis," and lunar rocks. Designed by Helmith, Obata and Cassabaum, this vast structure will open in 1976 and is the eastern-most of all the Smithsonian buildings.

A complete guide book is available at any Smithsonian shop.

OLD GLORY *(above right), the Hope Diamond (above left), and space cap-
sules (below left) share the spotlight in the various Smithsonian buildings on
the Mall. The red, sandstone castle (above) and the Hirshhorn Gallery (below
right) exemplify the different architectural styles in the Smithsonian complex.*

MERCURY SPACECRAFT
"Friendship 7"

(continued from page 71)

The most impressive and permanent addition to the city's cultural life was the bequest of an Englishman who had never been in this country. James Smithson willed his estate "to found at Washington, under the name of the Smithsonian Institution, an Establishment for the increase and diffusion of knowledge among men." In 1835 the nation inherited this windfall fortune of $550,000. John C. Calhoun sneezed: "It is beneath our dignity to accept presents from anyone." But John Quincy Adams disagreed: Congress would do itself a disservice if it were "palsied" by the will of the few. And for once, President Andrew Jackson and Adams agreed. Ideas of how to implement the inheritance included an astronomical observatory, a physical research lab, a university. In 1846, Congress finally decided on "a museum, an art gallery, a chemical laboratory and a library" — all in one. James Renwick's red stone Norman castle, with its Aesop towers, was erected in 1848, the first of numerous buildings. The Smithsonian's aegis broadened with the passing decades until it now shelters, among other bodies, the Freer Gallery of Oriental Art, the National Zoo, the National Museum of History and Technology, the new Air and Space Museum, and the Kennedy Center for the Performing Arts.

While the nation was expanding to fulfill its "manifest destiny," it endured many internal problems which were reflected in the capital. Congressman John Randolph, a Virginia slaveholder himself, decried "a crying shame before God and Man . . . [that there continued in operation] so infamous a slave market as in the metropolis, the seat of government of this nation which prides itself on freedom." Like other southern cities, Washington not only saw people auctioned, but enforced "black laws." These set evening curfews for free Negroes and required them to post good-conduct bonds signed by white sponsors. After *white* rioters destroyed many black homes in 1835, the price of a *black's* bond doubled to $1000, while persons of African ancestry who could not prove their free status were

A MODERN PARTHENON, *the porticoed Patent Office (now the home of the National Portrait Gallery) arose on F Street N.W. in 1836.*

jailed and sold into slavery. Despite this treatment — and despite wages that were generally half those paid whites — a strong middle class community of free blacks began to grow, centered around several churches.

Meanwhile, people were moving west to settle the Louisiana Purchase territories. As new states sought admission to the Union, the fragile balance between slave and free states was constantly debated, especially in the Senate. Adding to the political and emotional turmoil was the fact that each new state delegation further taxed the overcrowded Capitol. It was everybody's building. Congressmen mixed with peddlers selling wares in the rotunda, and Supreme Court Justices rubbed elbows with employees of the Library of Congress. Some new legislators set up rolltop desks in Capitol hallways or, like young Abraham Lincoln, rented boarding house rooms as offices. In time Congress acted to ease its congestion, appropriating money to add "ample accomodations for the two houses of Congress," *i.e.* two wings and the imposing dome seen today.

(continued on page 78)

PRIDES OF THE ANTEBELLUM CITY, *the Post Office (now the Tariff Commission, above) and the Patent Office (below) appear in 1846 daguerreotypes.*

FINALLY THE TALL DOME *of the Capitol began to rise above the clutter of war-time Pennsylvania Avenue (bottom), replacing the humbler early version (below).*

75

A City
of Universities

The historic dream of many that a "great national university" would arise on the capital's Mall never came to fruition. But Washington has become a major university center.

Washington's oldest university is Georgetown, with a present enrollment of about 10,000. Founded in 1789, it was America's first Catholic institution of higher learning. Its school of foreign service has educated many of this country's diplomats. Presidents, including George Washington, have spoken to the student body (more recently, the campus was featured in the film "The Exorcist").

George Washington University, the second oldest in the city, was founded in 1821 as the Columbian College in the District of Columbia. From its original setting in Mount Pleasant, the college moved to mid-town Washington and finally to its present location in Foggy Bottom. In the process, it changed its name to The George Washington University and became a degree-granting institution in all areas of academic endeavor. Today George Washington University has about 15,000 students in all of the arts and sciences. Its law and medical schools have particularly outstanding records.

Howard University in upper northwest Washington was founded shortly after the Civil War to provide education for former slaves and those previously prohibited from attending college by black laws. Named after General O.O. Howard who headed the Freedman's Bureau during the Civil War, the school has grown greatly — it now has a varied academic program including a school of architecture (the only one in the city) — and among its 9,000 students are citizens from all over the United States and the world.

The Catholic University of America, in the Brookland area of northeast Washington, is the only institution of higher learning in this country established under papal sponsorship. Beginning in 1889 as a Graduate School of the Sacred Sciences, it is now a complete university granting degrees from the B.A. to the Ph.D. Now, with almost 7,000 students, Catholic University is still closely affiliated with the Church. It has one of the best drama departments in the country — its university players are frequently called upon to give foreign tours during the summer.

The American University stands on the hill-top site of a Civil War fortress (Ft. Gains) in northwest Washington. Affiliated with the Methodist church and beset by many early hardships, the university succeeded in opening its doors to students in 1914. Using both the main campus and a subsequently developed downtown campus, the school grew quickly after WW I. Today a complete university, with over 15,000 students, American's School of International Service is one of the best in the country.

In 1964 the five universities in Washington and four smaller colleges — Gallaudet, Trinity, D.C. Teachers, and Mt. Vernon — joined in a "consortium" to make the resources of each available, in a gradual manner, to students of the other. The newest institution granting advanced degrees in Washington is the Federal City College, which opened its doors in 1968 and now has a total enrollment of over 5,000. Without a true campus yet, Federal City College was highly praised by the most recent board of accreditation and prospects for the first urban land grant college in the country look bright.

Thus, although Washington is not the home of "the National University," its numerous excellent schools make it one of the most distinguished academic neighborhoods in the world.

WASHINGTON'S UNIVERSITIES *are a point of pride in a city of culture. Above is Catholic University's new Hartke Theatre. Below, modern sculpture marks the home of American University. The statue at right (above) is of Thomas Gallaudet, founder of the first college for the deaf in the United States. George Washington University is justly proud of its new library (right) and the towers of Georgetown University's Healy Building (below, right) soar above the city on the Potomac palisades.*

(continued from page 75)

Typically for that troubled era, Washington became a city of divided loyalties. Many residents owned slaves but realized they were in an ambiguous situation: if the South should secede their city would remain capital of a northern nation opposed to the "peculiar institution." Firebrand Congressmen from North and South debated furiously. Many carried firearms. In 1856 Senator Charles Sumner of Massachusetts wrote a tract attacking slavery. Warned to tone down "the stinging force of language," he refused and was assaulted on the Senate floor by a rabid southern Congressman who caned Sumner unconscious. And even while Sumner's empty desk remained a testament to the passions of the times, a religious fanatic named John Brown briefly seized the Harpers Ferry Arsenal, about 50 miles from Washington, with the hopes of spurring a slave rebellion for freedom. He was executed for what he called "God's eternal truths" of emancipation and liberty and was beatified by Ralph Waldo Emerson as "that new saint." And slave owners everywhere shuddered, fearing that "John Brown's call for a slave uprising [might] be heard by their own. . . ." The country, the world, waited for a resolution of the crisis. In the fall of 1860, Abraham Lincoln was elected and southern states prepared to secede. One uncertainty vanished: the old compromises would no longer work.

As the new year, 1861, began, Pennsylvania Avenue dressed up for its sixteenth inauguration. Hotels like Brown's Palace and the Willard (a rambling barracks that filled nearly an entire block at 14th Street) were decked out in bunting. But the city wore a pall of worry, and many slave state Congressmen put on their traveling rags for the ultimate trip home. Secession had begun and the Confederate States of America adopted a provisional constitution on February 8. President James Buchanan did not act. On March 4, 1861 Lincoln was inaugurated. His address was moderate but firm: "The power confided in me will be used to hold, occupy and possess the property, and places belonging to the government . . . ." That was tantamount to equating secession with de facto rebellion. Despite frenzied conferences in the next weeks, the rift between North and South widened. Shortly before dawn on April 12, South Carolinians bombarded Fort Sumter in Charleston harbor, sparking the most destructive war in our history.

(continued on page 83)

PRESIDENT AND MRS. LINCOLN *appear below, portrayed shortly before the tragic end of his war-scarred administration.*

FORD'S THEATER *was hung with black crepe (top) after Lincoln's assassination there on April 14, 1865 during a performance of "Our American Cousin." Civil War artist Alfred Wand's sketch of the theater's interior (above) shows a figure at the spot to which assassin John Booth jumped after shooting the President in the box above. Today Ford's is once again a vital center for legitimate theater.*

Spires
of Worship
on
Washington's Skyline

Washington's religious diversity is clearly seen in the variety of its places of worship. Often called "the city of churches," it is one of the few American cities to include both a mosque (on Massachusetts Avenue just above Rock Creek Park) and a Greek Orthodox Cathedral, Saint Sophia, farther up Massachusetts Avenue. Almost next door to Saint Sophia stands the National Cathedral. This superb gothic building has been under construction since 1907. Like Westminster Abbey in London, it contains the remains of many of our nation's heroes, including President Woodrow Wilson, and Admiral George Dewey. Fulfilling George Washington's dream of a National Cathedral, it has served as home to five Christian denominations and a Jewish congregation as well as the headquarters of the Washington Episcopal Diocese in its long life.

Northeast Washington's skyline is dominated by the huge dome of the National Shrine of the Immaculate Conception, the largest Roman Catholic church in the country which took almost 40 years to complete. It is located on the campus of Catholic University. Nearby at 14th and Quincy Streets is the Franciscan Monastery of Washington. The monastery's catacombs are of particular interest, and the simulation of the stages of the cross provide for Catholics the same graces as a trip to the Holy Land.

Also among our famous religious structures is the Adas Israel Synagogue at 3rd and G Streets, N.W. Built in 1869, the synagogue is now being converted into a museum and the congregation has moved to the Adas Israel Synagogue at Connecticut and Porter Streets, N.W.

Thomas Circle, at 14th Street is the setting N.W., for the National City Church which is the Washington headquarters for the Disciples of Christ. Just around Thomas Circle is Luther Place Memorial Church built in 1870 by Washington Lutherans in thanksgiving for the end of the Civil War.

Patterned after the famed Saint Martins-in-the-field in London, the All Saints Unitarian Church was constructed northwest of Thomas Circle, near 16th Street and Harvard Square, in 1924. The nearby Church of the Latter Day Saints, built in 1933, is called "one of the most elegant small churches in the city" by the American Institute of Architects. Erected as a national memorial to religious liberty, the National Memorial Baptist Church was constructed in 1922 at 16th Street and Columbia Road. N.W. President Harry S Truman, recognizing the national importance of the New York Avenue Presbyterian Church, the church attended by several presidents including Lincoln, laid the cornerstone of the new building on the site of the old in 1951. Today the church contains an interesting collection of Lincolniana.

THE VITALITY OF RELIGION *has been a constant in Washington history — from the Gothic splendor of the National Cathedral (top right, opposite) to the neo-Byzantine style of the Shrine of the Immaculate Conception (top left). The 1876 drawing (below, opposite) shows black clerics demonstrating the importance of the church in Reconstruction Washington.*

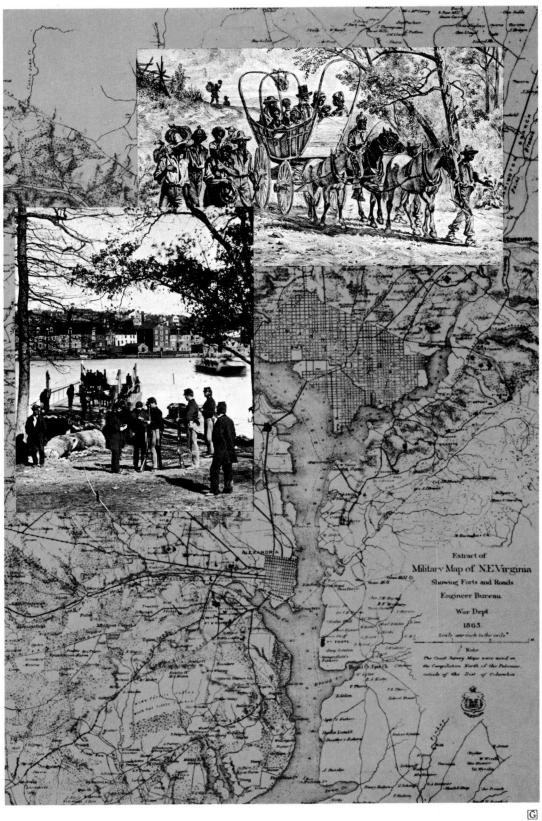

Extract of
Military Map of N.E.Virginia
Showing Forts and Roads
Engineer Bureau
War Dept
1865.
Scale one inch to the mile

(continued from page 78)

Almost overnight it transformed Washington. The slowly developing capital suddenly blossomed as a city of tents when soldiers flocked to their President's call. Maryland did not secede, so the capital was not surrounded. But Virginia, queen state of the Confederacy, lay across a river that had never seemed so narrow. The city was ringed with heavily-manned forts. Even so, a surprise raid by General Jubal Early and 15,000 battle hardened troops threatened the city in July 1864. Lincoln like many other Washingtonians went to see the fighting near Fort Stevens, on Seventh Street Road, now Georgia Avenue. Standing up to get a better view, he was grabbed by young Oliver Wendell Holmes. "Get down you fool," ordered the future Supreme Court Justice.

Troops filled every available building in Washington. The Capitol, its rotunda still unfinished, billeted several companies of soldiers early in the war. One recruit wrote home: "They gave us the Representatives chamber for quarters, the staff took the committee rooms and the Colonel the Speaker's Parlor." Several basement committee rooms became a bakery, fitted with ovens. Wrote the Secretary of the Interior: "The use of the crypt as a storage room [for flour] cuts off all direct communications between the two wings on that floor.

Many joined the army to wear the uniform. Arriving in Washington they were idle for months. Few expected the horrors of war. But on a hot Sunday in late July 1861, just thirty miles from Washington, at Bull Run, the war began in reality. Picnicking civilians watched as Confederate troops won that battle. As the ragged army of the Potomac began drilling for new battles, singing the mournful words of "John Brown's Body," a headstrong young woman from Boston named Julia Ward Howe was seized with emotion, and in the early light of dawn wrote the stirring words of the "Battle Hymn of the Republic."

As the war continued, Washington took on ever more the look of an army town. Government buildings became hospitals; livestock was corralled on the Mall; tent cities sprang up; brothels thrived. In the midst of this confusion, one of the Confederacy's most intriguing figures briefly reigned. A long-time Washington resident and ardent Dixie sympathizer, beautiful Rose O'Neal Greenhow pried information from important Yankee visitors to her attractive home on 16th Street, N.W., just opposite St. John's Church. Rose sent messages south telling of Union plans, unit strengths and schedules. When she was finally jailed in the Old Brick Capitol, the flow of information declined.

RINGED WITH FORTS, *Washington presented the image of a beleaguered citadel during the Civil War. The contemporary map (opposite) shows many of the forts' locations as well as the northern Virginia terrain over which the war raged. The superimposed scenes depict the area at war: blacks crossing the battle lines near Culpepper, Virginia and Union guards on Mason's Island across the Potomac from Georgetown.*

BRISTLING WITH GUNS, *Fort Stevens (where Lincoln heard enemy bullets sing) had recovered its composure by August, 1865 when the commemorative portrait at right was made.*

EMANCIPATION JUBILATION *greeted slavery's end (above). Blacks cele-brate in Washington in April, 1863.*

PEACE FOR ALL *on the banks of the Potomac was allegorized in the 1868 drawing below.*

In the midst of war, President Lincoln called for completion of the Capitol dome "as a symbol that our nation will go on." After the bloody battle of Antietam in September 1862, Lincoln saw the chance to make the symbol of freedom become a reality to all Americans. On January 1, 1863 "the Great Emancipator" issued the proclamation that freed all slaves in the rebellious states, in effect, all slaves in America. One former slave remembered years later: "Men squealed, women fainted, dogs barked, white and colored shook hands, songs were sung. It was indeed a time of times . . . Nothing like it will ever be seen again in this life."

To many, slavery was the root-cause of the war. James Russell Lowell viewed the South as a snake and: "It's slavery that's the fangs an 'thinkin' head/An' ef you want salvation cresh it dead." Lincoln's proclamation might have brought salvation, but it took Ulysses Grant and Lincoln's second election to beat the South and "cresh it dead." The poet Walt Whitman wrote in the later months of the war that "the toll of vast responsibilities, intricate questions, and demands of life and death cut deeper than ever upon [Lincoln's] dark brown face. . . . Yet all the old goodness, tenderness, sadness and canny shrewdness [remained] underneath the furrows. . . ."

A month after Lincoln's second inaugural General Robert E. Lee surrendered his proud Army of Northern Virginia. For most, the Civil War was over after Americans killed 630,000 Americans. Less than a week later, on April 14th, with the joy of triumph still in the air, President and Mrs. Lincoln went to Ford's Theatre on 10th Street to see a popular farce, "Our American Cousin." There, at the hands of John Wilkes Booth — a disturbed, romantic, southern sympathizer — he was assassinated. Booth was tracked down and killed. The conspirators who had assisted him were caught and summarily executed at Fort McNair, the beautiful army post in Southwest Washington.

In the gloom of "cheerless cold rain" of that suddenly peaceful but finally tragic April, Whitman wrote: "When lilacs last in the dooryard bloom'd, / And the great star early drop'd in the western sky in the night, / I mourned, and yet shall mourn with ever-returning spring."

Washington, city of national aspirations and triumphs, also learned how to wear the face of tragedy.

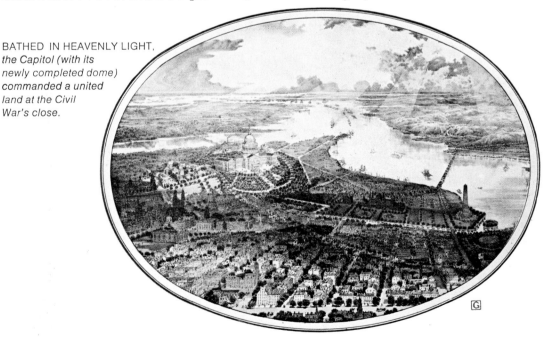

BATHED IN HEAVENLY LIGHT, *the Capitol (with its newly completed dome) commanded a united land at the Civil War's close.*

Washington's Gilded Age

The Civil War was over. The victory parades' martial music faded with the armies, armies that left behind them a drastically altered city.

The White House had suffered as much as any single building. It had been the Commander-in-Chief's headquarters, after all, a command post occasionally within earshot of combat. Its carpets were ruined by the boots and spurs of cavalry officers reporting to the President, its draperies tattered and its walls smeared.
Martha Patterson, President Andrew Johnson's daughter and official hostess, said: "We are plain people, Sir, from the mountains of Tennessee, and do not propose to put on airs." But she did mean to repair the damage and halt the dilapidation. By the time of General Ulysses S. Grant's inauguration in 1869, the mansion had an air of Victorian respectability.

Elsewhere, more was required than drapes and fresh paint. Shanty towns with intriguing names like Murder Bay, Swampoodle and Pipetown had mushroomed; now they remained squalid warrens where, stated a police report, "crime, filth and poverty

THE MAJESTY OF THE MALL *stretches from the foot of Capitol Hill to an imagined Washington Monument in the 1871 lithograph by Edward Sachse.*

seem to vie with each other in a career of degradation and death.'' Two policemen who went searching for a denizen of Murder Bay were never seen again.

The city's streets, little more than muddy tracks before the war, were far worse for the heavy wear of army wagon traffic. Gracious homes of southern sympathizers, many of them lions of pre-war society, had been confiscated and then fallen into disrepair. The old days were gone, and many who grieved them gone also, as the city turned its attention to the problems and opportunities of peace.

The conflict itself, its causes and results, had radically changed the fabric of America — by devastating the South, by priming the pumps of northern industry, by decimating a generation of men in both regions, by making all black people legally free. These changes did not mean total disruption. But there was a frantic reordering of priorities as freshly-vented energies sought new outlets and ambitious men sought new goals in the western territories, in eastern commerce and in the power seat of Washington where representatives of 36 states gathered.

Even as the White House was refurbished and the Capitol extended its wings over Jenkins Hill, voices in Congress renewed the call to move the government elsewhere. ''By a change of location of the Capital, the Government could rid itself of the great burdens imposed . . . by the present city,'' intoned one midwestern Member. Sympathies were strong for moving to a more geographically central place such as St. Louis.

The problems here were real indeed. Since 1802, Georgetown and the Federal City had been run by separate mayors and boards of aldermen while ''the County'' (meaning the rest of the District) was overseen by a Levy Court. Coordination among these bodies was limited at best and cooperation was nil since any creative improvements required money, and Congress always held the purse strings. The city was not an harmonious or creative

place as it recovered from the war. Horace Greeley, the cantankerous editor of the New York *Tribune* and a presidential candidate in 1872 groaned: ''The rents are high, the food is bad, the dust is disgusting, the mud is deep and the morals are deplorable.''

A real possibility that the government would evacuate spurred influential Washingtonians to action once again. The city had never become the commercial center George Washington imagined; its business was nothing but politics and — should the government vacate — it would be as if the Mississippi had suddenly abandoned New Orleans. The District of Columbia would become a ghost town with a dead economy, a ruination for men like W.W. Corcoran. Son of a Georgetown mayor, he had taken advantage of this country's confused financial structure in the 1830s and 1840s to become a millionaire. When the Civil War began he sent more than a million dollars in gold to England for safekeeping and went himself to Paris. Returning to Washington, he realized both his wealth and influence depended on the city's prosperity. Though a dyed-in-the-wool Democrat, he joined forces with resident Republicans to advance their mutual self-interest on Capitol Hill. In an era that saw the birth of modern lobbying — the employment of paid professionals by special interests to bend the ears of legislators — Corcoran and his temporary allies fought with every weapon they could muster. They won.

In 1871, after months of bickering, Congress decided to stay and to install a new form of local government designed to solve the most obvious problems. It bound the three jurisdictions into a single unit that was to be governed like one of the western territories (but of course no one intended it to achieve statehood, since Congress still meant to rule its own roost). The President would appoint a governor, the council and various boards; local residents would elect a legislative assembly and a non-voting delegate to the House of Representatives. This period of territorial rule was brief but immensely important to the city's solidification and growth — largely because of one man, Alexander R. Shepherd. Appointed as a member of the Board of Public Works, Shepherd's power soon eclipsed that of the governor. "Why is the new governor like a sheep?" asked a columnist in one of the dozen-odd daily newspapers. "Because he is led by A. Shepherd," came the reply, containing more than a kernel of truth.

Son of a lumber dealer, Shepherd had been born in southwest Washington and had started fending for himself early, his father having died when he was ten. Caught up in the popular pre-war militancy, he joined the National Rifles, a militia group that made the first raid into Dixie — an inconsequential foray in 1861 across the Potomac's Long Bridge at the foot of 14th Street. His three-month enlistment up, he mustered out before the Battle of Bull Run to return to his civilian work as a plumbing contractor. Like many behind the lines, he emerged from the war rich. A big, burly, expansive man, Shepherd was devoted to his large family and popular among his many friends. By the age of 36 his influence in business circles matched that of Corcoran who was twice his age. He was into everything: He founded eating clubs, supported the New York Avenue Presbyterian Church, promoted the Jefferson Nine (baseball flowered during the Civil War). Director of both a bank and an insurance company, he had interests in railroads, streetcars, markets, real estate, construction firms and *The Evening Star*. He was even a leading member of the newly formed Association for the Prevention of Cruelty to Animals.

Named to the Board of Public Works by his friend President Grant, he invented the position Vice-President of the Board and promoted himself into it. He took it upon himself — and upon his like-minded associates — to re-do the city in a spectacular manner. Not only did this clique have a financial stake in things, they took great pride in their hometown. Those who opposed their plans, Shepherd said, should "get up and git."

The Secretary of the Smithsonian warned that the canal running along the Mall would breed malarial mosquitos. Since it hadn't brought much business anyway, Shepherd filled it in. At 17th Street and Constitution Avenue still stands a stone building which was a canal lock house. Shepherd leveled entire hills to construct a sewer system that was to make Washington one of the most sanitary cities of this time. He planted 60,000 trees, paved streets, installed street lights, and one dark night he tore up a railroad track crossing Pennsylvania Avenue below Capitol Hill. Other railways remained, but a local poet chortled triumphantly: "That Shepherd who tends his flocks by night / For he needeth no light of day / To change the grade of a street or walk / Or to move a railroad away." The changes were as enormous as Shepherd's appetite. Two Senators returning from a summer recess found their homes "poised on the brink of an ochre-colored abyss, while laborers toiled below in a wilderness of sewers and half-laid sidewalks."

FLOCKING TO THE CAPITOL, *politicians and petitioners after the Civil War struggled with the first civil rights legislation.*

G

J

J

THE RECONSTRUCTION ERA *is symbolized by the folk painting below. The harsh reality of the era was personified by Frederick Douglass (above, left) who had been born in slavery and rose to leadership of the civil libertarian cause. Until 1877 he lived on Capitol Hill (in a house now occupied by The Museum of African Art (above); then he moved to "Cedar Hill," a gracious residence in Anacostia (left), now operated by the National Parks.*

L

Inevitably, not everyone was pleased. Concentrating improvements in northwest neighborhoods, Shepherd earned the particular enmity of speculators and builders who had invested in land on Capitol Hill. Meanwhile, eyebrows were raised at how much money he was spending: some $20 million, $10 million more than authorized. Things were getting done that had needed doing for decades, but through the billowing dust of various projects appeared shadows of fiscal impropriety if not actual graft. Still, Shepherd had Grant's confidence and the improvements continued even after complaints forced Congress to investigate. The President told Congress: "I recommend a liberal policy . . . the government should pay its just share of the expenses for these improvements."

Cries of corruption, many of them well founded, became stronger. One critic went so far as to say: "It can be proved that Mr. Alexander R. Shepherd . . . went to New York . . . to take lessons of Boss Tweed," the notorious leader of Tamany Hall. Another investigation was begun. No specific wrongdoing on Shepherd's part was ever proved, but that may have been because "the Boss" had powerful friends in Congress. Still, Congress decided it had had enough of territorial government and headstrong local officials. The experiment in limited self-government for the District came to an abrupt end in 1874; thereafter Washington residents lost all political prerogatives for nearly a century. Robbed of all rights to vote — District residents had been barred from presidential elections

DECORATING THE HILL, *artists and architects built elaborate confections such as the Bartholdi Fountain (wreathed by ladies, above) and mansarded houses such as the Frederick Douglass Capitol Hill home at left.*

from the start — they were now to be governed by a board of commissioners whom the President appointed and removed at will. These commissioners, in turn, followed the dictates of Congressional committees which continued to clench the purse.

Besmirched by gossip and unproved charges, Shepherd later filed for bankruptcy and left Washington for Mexico. Only a few years later he emerged as a millionaire there too and lived regally till his death from appendicitis in 1902.

If he had neglected Capitol Hill, Shepherd had done well by the area near the junction of Massachusetts and Connecticut Avenues where he had built three houses. Barely a decade earlier this territory had been described gloomily by English novelist Anthony Trollope: ''Go there and you will find yourself . . . in an uncultivated, undrained wilderness. Tucking your trousers up to your knees, you will wade through bogs; you will lose yourself among the rude hillocks; you will be out of reach of humanity. A stranger finds himself . . . wading through snipe grounds, looking for civilization where none exists.'' That junction soon had its corners rounded to become Dupont Circle, hub of one of Washington's poshest neighborhoods for decades and, in recent years, a busy gathering place — for chess players, folk singers, sun bathers, marchers and idlers around its marble fountain.

(continued on page 98)

UPON THE PARKS *and circles of Washington in the Gilded Age and after arose monuments to heroes such as Admiral Samuel DuPont (above) and the men of World War I's First Division (right).*

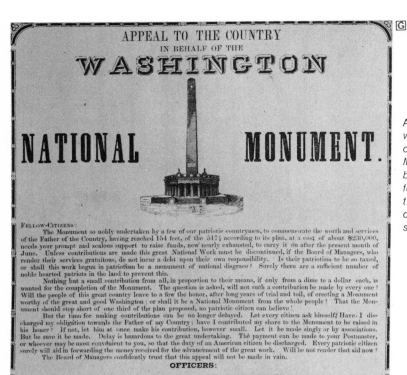

APPEAL TO THE COUNTRY
IN BEHALF OF THE
WASHINGTON
NATIONAL   MONUMENT.

FELLOW-CITIZENS:

The Monument so nobly undertaken by a few of our patriotic countrymen, to commemorate the worth and services of the Father of the Country, having reached 154 feet, of the 517½ according to its plan, at a cost of about $230,000, needs your prompt and zealous support to raise funds, now nearly exhausted, to carry it on after the present month of June. Unless contributions are made this great National Work must be discontinued, if the Board of Managers, who render their services gratuitous, do not incur a debt upon their own responsibility. Is their patriotism to be so taxed, or shall this work begun in patriotism be a monument of national disgrace? Surely there are a sufficient number of noble hearted patriots in the land to prevent this.

Nothing but a small contribution from all, in proportion to their means, if only from a dime to a dollar each, is wanted for the completion of the Monument. The question is asked, will not such a contribution be made by every one? Will the people of this great country leave to a few the honor, after long years of trial and toil, of erecting a Monument worthy of the great and good Washington; or shall it be a National Monument from the whole people? That the Monument should stop short of one third of the plan proposed, no patriotic citizen can believe?

But the time for making contributions can be no longer delayed. Let every citizen ask himself, Have I discharged my obligation towards the Father of my Country; have I contributed my share to the Monument to be raised in his honor? If not, let him at once make his contribution, however small. Let it be made singly or by associations. But be sure it be made. Delay is hazardous to the great undertaking. The payment can be made to your Postmaster, or whoever may be most convenient to you, so that the duty of an American citizen be discharged. Every patriotic citizen surely will aid in forwarding the money received for the advancement of the great work. Will he not render that aid now?

The Board of Managers confidently trust that this appeal will not be made in vain.

OFFICERS:

FRANKLIN PIERCE, *President of the United States, and ex-officio President.*
ARCH. HENDERSON, *First Vice President.*
JOHN T. TOWERS, *Mayor of Washington, and ex-officio Second Vice President.*
THOS. CARBERRY, *Third Vice President.*
J. B. H. SMITH, *Treasurer.*

MANAGERS:

WINFIELD SCOTT,
N. TOWSON,
PETER FORCE,
W. W. SEATON,
W. A. BRADLEY,
W. W. CORCORAN,
P. R. FENDALL,
ELISHA WHITTLESEY·

A PATRIOTIC FUND DRIVE *was launched in 1854 to complete the Washington Monument. Begun in 1848 but halted by insufficient funds and political turmoil, the monument stood for decades as a reproachful stump on the Mall.*

A PINNACLE FOR THE AGES, *the Washington Monument projects the towering leadership of the First President. Though visitors once could walk up its 555 feet, now all must ride the elevator (time: 70 seconds).*

A QUESTION OF DESIGN *troubled the monument's builders even after archi-*
tect Robert Mills' entry (above left) won the nation-wide competition in 1836.
Later suggestions were as bizarre as the English gothic non-church above, right.

AN ATTENTION TO DETAIL *was lavished on the monument when work recom-*
menced in 1878. The solid aluminum tip (below left) having been set in place,
opening ceremonies were held on February 21, 1885 (below right).

Washington's Beautiful Embassies

Nothing symbolizes Washington's impact on foreign affairs so much as the numerous embassies here. More than any other capital city, Washington is home to diplomats from all over the world. Generally each country has two buildings that together constitute the embassy: the chancery, where the offices are maintained, and the ambassador's residence, which is used in addition to living space, for entertainment. Usually, these buildings are in close proximity to one another, sometimes actually neighboring.

As different as the countries represented here are the buildings that serve as embassies. Some countries prefer today's modernistic design, such as the interesting Brazilian Embassy at 3006 Massachusetts Avenue, N.W. or the West German Embassy at 4645 Reservoir Road, N.W. More traditional architectural styles are also sometimes desired as seen in the Turkish Embassy at 1603 23rd Street, N.W. or the beautiful, turn-of-the-century Indonesian Embassy at 2020 Massachusetts Avenue, N.W.

Called Embassy Row in honor of its numerous foreign residents, N.W. Massachusetts Avenue is probably the most cosmopolitan avenue in any city of the world. The first to build there were the British in 1928 and their embassy at 3100 has grown through the years. The British are particularly proud of the statue of Sir Winston Churchill which stands forth on Massachusetts Avenue with a confident look holding in his ''V'' crooked fingers the famed cigar.

For many visitors, particularly those lucky few invited to parties there, the Japanese Embassy at 2516 Massachusetts Avenue is a particular delight, since behind the chancery building is a beautiful ceremonial tea house.

Many embassies in Washington were built as private residences. The Canadian Embassy, 1746 Massachusetts Avenue, for example, was first occupied by Mrs. Axel Wichfeld, heiress to the Swift Packing fortune, and her first husband Clarence Moore.

Another embassy that was built as a private residence is the Russian Embassy at 1115 16th Street, N.W. Built for the widow of George Pullman, the developer of the Pullman Sleeping Coach, it was purchased by the Russians in 1913. The Russians do not have the only embassy on 16th Street. In fact, so numerous are the embassies on this avenue that it is often referred to as ''Little Embassy Row.'' The Italians take great pride in their structure, which they say represents the ornamental decorations of Venice, the artistic value of Florence, and the historical worths of Rome.

Other countries represented are quartered in areas from Cleveland Park, to the Kalorama area, but each embassy adds its own spice to the flavor of Washington.

EMBASSY ROW *where the world's elite meet, is as varied in architecture as in people. The Iranian embassy (opposite, top) has an exotic Middle-Eastern look. The Brazilian Embassy (middle) is international-modern, while the Embassy of Japan (bottom) follows traditional lines.*

PRESIDENTIAL STYLE *waxed fancy at the turn of the century. The interior of the White House during Harrison's administration (top) was smothered in plush. Pictures of the period show two of Theodore Roosevelt's children. Alice (left) and Kermit (above at left).*

G

Z

PRESIDENTIAL MOODS *have changed with the advancing eras. McKinley's White House aides (above) seem embalmed forever in the stiff collar and pince-nez of their day. President Ford seems considerably less formal, though still possessed of his mighty office's panoply.*

(continued from page 91)

Shepherd's speculation prompted others to follow, like the "California Syndicate" or the "honest Miners' Group." One of their still surviving extravagances was the home of House Speaker James G. Blaine, who lost the election of 1884 to Grover Cleveland. An imposing redbrick mansion with a deep porch and jutting chimneys at 20th Street and Massachusetts Avenue, it has changed with the neighborhood. Its upper floors have been converted to offices and its back has served as everything from a grocery store to a bicycle shop. Farther up Massachusetts Avenue a millionaire named Curtis J. Hillyer built the stone mansion across from the Society of the Cincinnati. The Hillyer residence is now the prestigious Cosmos Club. A block away, General Sheridan's equestrian statue at the circle bearing his name marks the foot of Embassy Row. More than two dozen foreign missions, some old some new, line the avenue between here and the Naval Observatory, which is now the Vice President's official residence.

But before any of this could be built, the "briars and rabbit burrows" had to be eliminated and the marshes drained. It had taken a man like Shepherd to start the job of filling in gullies fifty feet deep and aligning the bluff commanding Rock Creek Valley that would become Massachusetts Avenue. Boundary Street, formerly the outer limit of urban living, became Florida Avenue. The Kalorama Estate, owned by a succession of affluent families, was progressively diminished by sales of house lots to speculators. The wife of a British diplomat was so pleased with her new surroundings that she called it "Washington's Mayfair," a complimentary comparison to one of London's most exclusive areas. When Woodrow Wilson left the White House he moved to a house at S Street and Massachusetts near today's Textile Museum. Herbert Hoover lived only a few doors away until he moved to 1600 Pennsylvania Avenue in 1929.

Among the most elegant and exotic exteriors found in this area are the residence of the French ambassador and the modern Islamic Center and Mosque. These properties overlook Rock Creek Park, which here is a verdant chasm. In the

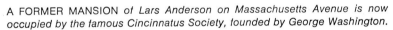

A FORMER MANSION of Lars Anderson on Massachusetts Avenue is now occupied by the famous Cincinnatus Society, founded by George Washington.

1890's Rock Creek Park was just taking shape as the largest public park within the confines of any American city. It was designed as a "pleasuring ground for the benefit and enjoyment of the people of the United States," a promise it fulfills today.

To the east another important neighborhood began to grow. Meridian Hill, so named because it was the city's highest point on the 77th meridian, was the original site of George Washington University. It was sparsely settled until after the Civil War when the presence of the college, the pressure of the city's population and transportation contributed to its growth. Amid scattered mansions middle class neighborhoods grew, inhabited largely by the burgeoning number of government workers. Like many other outlying parts in the late 19th century, Meridian Hill was almost a small town unto itself. It even had its own eccentric poet in Joaquim Miller, the self-styled "Byron of the Sierras." Seeking a familiar setting, Miller built a rustic log cabin on the hill, a copy of western mountain dwellings. Some years later it was moved to Rock Creek Park where it remains a tourists' curiosity.

Still farther east, Le Droit Park was one of Washington's first planned suburban communities with a distinctive architectural style. The proximity to Howard University (the nation's outstanding academy for recently freed slaves) made this area particularly appealing to the academic faculty. It became, and to a degree has remained, the focal point for Washington's growing black intelligentsia.

Frederick Douglass, the civil libertarian, was the most celebrated black in the city of the time. "The Sage of Anacostia" adopted Washington during the war years; his home, Cedar Hill, was the scene of many social gatherings for elite blacks and whites and remains a public shrine maintained by the National Park Service. His earlier residence in town is now the celebrated Museum of African Art at 316 A Street, N.E. Despite his growing disappointment that the nation failed to make emancipation a social and economic reality, Douglass defended its capital: "It is our national center. It belongs to us, and whether it is

(continued on page 102)

TO THE SOCIETY *belong first sons of families tracing descent from officers of the Revolution. Two of its grand spaces appear opposite and below.*

Aquatic Attractions

Built in Maryland's tidewater region, early Washington was often victimized by the mighty Potomac's spring floods. Throughout the season, 19th century residents complained of the bogs and marshes. Now, rather than a liability, the abundance of water is a distinct esthetic and recreational advantage.

The Potomac River provides a happy fishing grounds in the spring during the shad and herring runs, and hooks are dropped for other fish in all months of the year. The June running of the President's Cup Regatta speed boat race brings large crowds. For those who like less dangerous aquatic adventures, several marinas and boat houses have everything from small sail boats to canoes for rent.

The beautiful Chesapeake and Ohio Canal, which parallels the Potomac to Cumberland, Maryland, was begun in 1828 and finally completed in 1850. Never a major money maker, the C & O nevertheless continued in operation as a transporter of grain, coal and produce, until a major storm destroyed much of it in 1924. By this time the canal was owned by the Baltimore and Ohio Railroad which turned the entire 154-mile canal over to the federal government in payment of a $2,000,000 debt in 1938. The Park Service oversaw the development of the canal into one of the East Coast's most attractive park areas. The museum at Great Falls is of particular interest. The towpath is a lure to bicyclists and joggers in the spring, summer and fall, while canoes and rowboats provide easy transportation through the canal's calm water. And in winter the canal is mobbed by skaters anxious to show their skills. In 1972, Hurricane Agnes did much damage to the canal which the Park Service is presently repairing. Soon the always popular canal boat trips will once again be available from Georgetown to Little Falls, five miles away.

It is possible to get a graphic idea of the general marshiness of parts of Washington by visiting the Kenilworth Aquatic Gardens in extreme northeast Washington. The gardens, begun in 1882 as a hobby by a government clerk named W.B. Chase, came under Park Service control in 1938. The marshland in which many beautiful and exotic plants now grow (including the Egyptian lotus, supposedly Cleopatra's favorite), is only slightly altered from its original condition by dikes which separate the numerous ponds. Summer is the best time for viewing the beautiful aquatic plants — the croaking of bull frogs and swamp crickets is virtually symphonic at that time.

By 1976 the Mall will include other watery attractions. A six-acre lake, which will include a small island accessible by a footbridge will be the primary point of interest in a forty-five-acre park. Ducks, geese and fish will thrive in the lake. The lake, combined with the already existing reflecting pool, and skating rink will give this section of the Mall some of the formality dreamed of by Washington's water loving planners.

LOVELY LILIES FLOWER *all summer in the beautiful Kenilworth Aquatic Gardens.*

J

SHIP AHOY *calls a weekend sailor as he approaches one of Washington's*
many marinas (above). [J]

MIRRORED IN WATER, *the historic Cabin John Bridge (below) was a master-*
piece of engineering by Montgomery Meigs and Jefferson Davis.

[G]

(continued from page 99)

mean or majestic, whether arrayed in glory or covered with shame, we cannot but share its character and its destiny.''

Washington was indeed becoming a national center that mirrored myriad aspects of the changing American character. Mark Twain saw its ostentious displays of wealth as ''dreariness, flimsiness and bad taste reduced to mathematical completeness,'' just as the late 19th century indulged in the first orgy of conspicuous consumption. But others felt ostentation marked the height of gentility. Two women typified the conflicting spirits of these times.

After Rutherford B. Hayes won the disputed election of 1876, his wife announced that the White House should have nothing in common with a saloon. ''Lemonade Lucy,'' as the press dubbed this Calvinistic First Lady, declared she would not serve demon rum in her home. Washingtonians, raised on ''poker, politics and punch,'' were appalled; but they were not to be denied for long. After a little coaxing, White House libationists concocted ''Roman Punch'' — oranges filled with a frozen

recipe that was largely alcoholic. It became an enormous hit and while the table that served it was openly called ''the life-saving station,'' Mrs. Hayes never questioned why oranges became so popular.

Kate Chase Sprague, daughter of a Chief Justice and wife of a millionaire Senator, personified the other Washington society in the ''gilded age.'' Brilliant, witty, ambitious, affectionate, she engaged in affairs that were the talk of the town. Her obvious connection with the handsome senator from New York, Roscoe Conkling, drove her husband to fits of jealousy. Once in Newport, Rhode Island, where Washington's wealthiest spent summers, Senator Sprague chased Senator Conkling down the main street brandishing a gun while his prey tripped over his suspenders.

Meanwhile, the business of government had expanded and the executive branch had outgrown its quarters. The spectacular edifice now standing next door to the White House was begun in 1871 to accommodate the State, War and Navy Departments. Today is the imposing Executive Office

SNOWBOUND *residents of Washington slog through drifts after the century's worst snowfall in 1922 (below left). Hurricane Agnes provided dramatic pictures and high waters in 1972.*

G   J

Building. The building brought immediate response. Some called Architect A.B. Mullet a "second Michelangelo," while Henry Adams dubbed the building an "architectural infant asylum."

Before the war, W.W. Corcoran had commissioned James Renwick, the designer of the original Smithsonian castle, to build an art gallery across the street from Mullet's architectural *tour de force*. Renwick's understated architectural gem proved too small, so the present Corcoran Gallery of Art at the corner of New York Avenue and 17th Street, N.W. was constructed in 1892. The original building was a courthouse for a time, then a warehouse. Almost razed in the 1960s, the Renwick Gallery is now a showcase for American design under the Smithsonian's widespread aegis.

Hopes of giving Washington a truly ceremonial appearance were revived with the resumption of work on the Washington Monument. Central to L'Enfant's all-but-forgotten plan, it had been begun in 1848. The nearby canal and marshy ground had made work difficult; lack of money made it next to impossible; the "Pope's stone episode" brought construction to a standstill in 1854. Like every state of the union, many private organizations and most foreign powers, the Vatican had sent a piece of masonry to be included in the structure. But anti-Catholic prejudice was running high, and a band of bigots stole the stone one midnight and heaved it into the Potomac. This heated controversy was the last straw; until the territorial period, the monument remained a stub. Once resumed, work progressed slowly as the foundations were strengthened. Finally on a blustery February day in 1885, the completed shaft was dedicated — at 555 feet the tallest structure then standing in the world.

The view from the top was one of extremes. In the foreground, train sheds and railroad yards disfigured L'Enfant's planned formal gardens. Beyond, nature and intelligence seemed to have won the battle against ugliness and stupidity. Graceful terraces led magnificently up to the Capitol. Designed by Frederick Law Olmstead (planner of New York's Central

(continued on page 108)

FLOODED *Pennsylvania Avenue stalled carriages in 1889. Washington's weather remains wet, but engineers have minimized flooding.*

G

MEMORIALS TO HEROES *both humble and famed dot the Washington landscape. Below, a soldier stands watch over the Tomb of the Unknowns also in Arlington Cemetery.*

E

SAILORS AND SOLDIERS *muster on the steps of the Jefferson Memorial (above) and citizens gather in front of the John Kennedy gravesite at Arlington Cemetery (bottom right). The Seamen's Memorial along the George Washington Parkway is a study in balance and grace (bottom left).*

Sculpture's Grand Display

From the truly sublime to the nearly ridiculous, Washington's outdoor art ranges the breadth of creativity. The massive and impressive Grant Memorial at the base of Capitol Hill, designed and largely sculpted by Henry Shrady, includes the second largest equestrian statue in the world. Washington also boasts the "Temperance Fountain" on Pennsylvania Avenue at 8th Street — it is not a fountain, and is located directly in front of a liquor store. Thus the monuments here reflect in various ways the hopes and dedications of us all.

Lafayette Park holds statues of foreigners at each corner: Lafayette, on the southeast corner; Jean Baptiste Rochambeau on the southwest corner; Thaddeus Kosciusko on the northeast corner; Freidrich von Steuben on the northwest corner. Although Washington has no Statue of Liberty, it has a magnificent piece by the same French artist, Frederich Bartholdi. An outstanding example of foreign aid received by the United States, the beautiful Bartholdi Fountain stands opposite the Botanic Gardens on Independence Avenue.

One of Washington's most interesting areas for statuary is Meridian Hill Park. Here a bronze representation of President James Buchanan by Hans Schuler stands near a statue of Dante, the great Italian poet. And in the same is a replica of the equestrian statue of Joan of Arc which long stood before the cathedral in Rheims, France.

The seated statue "Serenity" also in Meridian Hill Park, brings to mind August St. Gauden's beautiful piece "Grief" in Rock Creek Cemetary west of North Capitol Street, just past the Soldier's Home. It was to this statue, sculpted in memory of Henry Adams's wife that Eleanor Roosevelt frequently travelled to gain peace in her first stay in Washington during WW I. Eleanor's husband, F.D.R. is simply memoralized by a marble block in the little triangle in front of the Archives Building. Roosevelt himself selected the spot, and stipulated that his memorial be small and plain.

Wherever one walks in the city one encounters American heroes in modern or classical guise. The tall, spare, Taft Carillon on Constitution Avenue half way up Capitol Hill, recalls Robert Taft, known to history as one of the Senate's "big five." Not far away, at Union Station, a distant relative of Robert Taft's, Larado Taft, designed the Columbus Memorial Fountain which salutes the explorer who is credited with discovering our land. And in Lincoln Park at North Capitol and 12th Streets, the National Park Service recently unveiled Robert Berkes' excellent statue of Mary McCleod Bethune, the great black educator.

Certainly the most antique monument in the city is the exquisite Japanese Lantern on the Tidal Basin. Sculpted in the 17th century, it welcomes many new visitors to Washington each year when a ceremonial lighting marks the traditional beginning of the annual Cherry Blossom Festival.

MAYOR WALTER WASHINGTON *and representatives from Japan ignite the sculpted lantern at Cherry Blossom time.*

[J]

AN OUTSTANDING LEADER, *black educator Mary Bethune stands above young admirers. Her statue sculpted by Robert Berkes, was unveiled in Lincoln Park in 1974.*

[G]

A SEATED WASHINGTON, *the work of neo-classical sculptor Horatio Greenough was originally placed in the Capitol's rotunda. Deemed improper there, it was moved to the Capitol's East Front (above). Later it was removed (below) to the Smithsonian—where it remains a curiosity piece.*

[G]

(continued from page 103)

Park, and contributor to the National Zoo in Rock Creek Park), the terraces were the early site for annual Easter egg rolls.

Across the river stood the stately Curtis-Lee Mansion, once Robert E. Lee's home, designed by the same George Hadfield who had designed the first City Hall (now the District Court House) on D Street, N.W. The mansion now guards Arlington National Cemetery where the remains of soldiers of all the nation's wars and of Presidents Taft and Kennedy rest. To the north, the bustling city was taking shape, filling out in a manner that reflected the nation's growth and wealth in the age of industrial robber barons and city bosses. And Mark Twain remarked, if the new wealth was ''acquired by conspicuous ingenuity with just a pleasant little spice of illegality, all the better.''

Behind the wide vistas and gleaming new facades there was squalor. As the century progressed, dreams of black equality faded. The city that had been a beacon to freedom-seeking slaves now held thousands of hidden slums. ''Alley dwellings'' cowered in the center of many city blocks that were rimmed with respectable homes. They would remain until the 1930s when their residents moved to other slums.

But for middle class people, the town was recovering its southern grace and paces. Picturesque rides were available on numerous street railways. If it still took nearly an hour to cross Rock Creek gorge, an easy excursion could be made to the zoo (now home of Smokey the Bear and the pandas given by the People's Republic of China). For those seeking open country, pastoral settings remained within streetcar ride distance until long after WW I. These rural areas continued to produce much of the food sold in many-stalled markets. One of these, the Eastern Market at 7th and C Streets, S.E., plies its varied trade today.

But the Mall was still an ugly train depot. Despite even the dynamic Shepherd's efforts, a station remained on the site now occupied by the National Gallery of Art. It

was here in July 1881 that President James Garfield was shot by a disappointed office-seeker. Although one heard constant complaints about the station, Congress even suggested in 1900 that this Pennsylvania Railroad barn be expanded to accommodate other lines. It would ''add greatly to the beauty of that portion of the mall'' proclaimed Michigan Senator James McMillan, who nonetheless acquiesced ultimately to the concept of city planning, a science of growing popularity. Congress appointed a committee to examine the whole problem of central Washington and the Mall. Its chairman was the brilliant Daniel H. Burnham, who had designed the Chicago Columbian Exhibition in 1893. His rule of thumb was: ''Make no small plans. They have no power to move men's souls.'' He was empowered to design a model for ''the Park System of the District of Columbia'' and bring the city as a whole in closer line with L'Enfant's original vision.

The McMillan Commission's plan called for construction of Union Station northeast of the Capitol. It would be used by all the railroads. In 1902 this blueprint was endorsed by Alexander Cassatt, president of the Pennsylvania Railroad and brother of Mary Cassatt, the nation's foremost impressionist painter. He agreed to vacate the Mall and occupy the Burnham-designed, vaulted neoclassical building

TRANSPORTATION IN A CHANGING WORLD *reflects the developing community. The 1890's open air street-cars (opposite) are gone, as are their 1910 descendants (below). The newest addition to public transportation on the roadways is the Metro Midi-bus (right).*

presently undergoing renovation to the National Visitors Center.

The new Mall would be lined with government buildings and terminate in a "temple" to President Lincoln on land reclaimed from the Potomac. A new sea wall would finally end the area's frequent flooding. Hearing of this, House Speaker Joseph "Uncle Joe" Cannon railed "I'll never let a memorial to Abraham Lincoln be erected in a g—d— swamp" since it would "shake itself down with loneliness and ague." His suggestion for a Virginia site met stiff opposition and the original plan progressed to include Memorial Bridge which would lead across the river to Arlington National Cemetery.

Though formality was the watchword, the Commission also noted that "the dearth of means of innocent enjoyment of one's leisure hours is remarkable." It called for ball fields and the Tidal Basin was complemented with "facilities for boating and for wading and swimming in the summer as well as for skating in the winter." Among the new buildings built under this plan were the Cannon and Russell buildings, the first separate House and Senate office structures.

Slowly the Mall was transformed and newspaper writers waxed poetic. "The grandeur of the city told the world 'It shall be mine [Washington's] to teach thee the meaning and . . . the soul of the beauty that lies within.'" These were idyllic years.

But in Detroit, young Henry Ford was developing a method for mass-producing a machine that would crush the human-scaled assumptions on which city planning then rested. The automobile vastly extended the distances a person could easily travel by private means. Like Prometheus's fire, it was a useful tool and toy that would also bring peril and not a little destruction. It totally reordered commerce, working habits and residential development. In May 1896 a circus parade brought the first car to drive down Pennsylvania Avenue. Few onlookers realized what changes would chug along in its wake.

A BROODING LINCOLN *presides in the center of the august, porticoed me-morial dedicated to him in 1922 and designed by Daniel Chester French.*

A Capital
For The
World

Theodore Roosevelt personified America as it stampeded into the twentieth century. The rough riding advocate of the "strenuous life" brought his rollicking crew to the White House after William McKinley's assassination in 1901. The Victorian mustiness was cleared from the staid old mansion as the building was altered in form and spirit. The greenhouses that grew flowers for First Ladies' tables were removed; a new east entrance was built and the west wing extended. The refurbished White House made a "bully pulpit" said the man who some claimed wanted to be "the bride at every wedding and the corpse at every funeral."

This first family stirred the city with its antics. The Roosevelt boys, all four of them, ran riot through the mansion, and their beautiful sister, dubbed "Princess Alice . . . the belle of Washington" married House Speaker Nicholas Longworth in the East Room. For one day at least, the President took a back seat. A tornado of a man with far flung interests, Roosevelt showed keen concern with the

CHERRY TREES *burst forth in blossom each April to break winter's icy grip on the Tidal Basin by the Jefferson Memorial (below) and to welcome a new freshet of tourists to Washington.*

J

growth and development of the city and studied carefully the plans developed by the McMillan commission. Continued White House interest in the city was demonstrated by Helen Taft (wife of the rotund twenty-seventh President) who encouraged the planting of the Japanese cherry trees around the Tidal Basin.

The tracks were gone from the Mall, and the cherry trees ringing the Tidal Basin with their generous blossoms made Washington its small city best just at the outbreak of World War I. Tree-shaded boulevards and elegant residences combined to make it seem a prosperous rural seat. Its growing public and private institutions made it a center of genteel intellectuality and bright diversion. Henry James called Washington "the city of conversation," and Helen Nicolay, daughter of one of Lincoln's secretaries, noted that here "there is always something new under the sun." When the war came the pace quickened. Then "the one invariable rule seemed to be that every individual was found doing something he or she never dreamed of doing before. The rule worked even in those somnolent parts of Georgetown that seemed under the spell of a Rip Van Winkle sleep."

The days immediately preceding our entry into World War I were more frenzied than those prior to the conflict a half-century earlier. Hotel bellhops drilled after hours and thousands of Boy Scouts announced their preparedness to mobilize instantly for "first aid work, police and detective duty." Congress' declaration of war launched the American Expeditionary Force to Europe in 1917 and summoned armies of civilians to Washington in search of romance, adventure and jobs. They flocked to do their part to win the war that would "make the world safe for democracy." Wrote one witness: "Young women arrived by every train to do 'war work,' coming with the magnificent trustfulness of youth without a thought as to where they should lodge or how they were to be fed." Older Washingtonians grumbled and compared these new arrivals to common pests. In a year the city had 200,000 new residents.

Boarding houses, hotels, even private homes were crammed with transients while a teeming corps of fledgling bureau-

The Government asks you to do your Xmas Shopping Early
DO IT NOW

[G]

PATRIOTISM *during World War I urged workers to get their jobs done swiftly— to be "Minute Men."*

4 Minute Men

A Message from The Government at Washington

COMMITTEE ON PUBLIC INFORMATION

[G]

crats created blizzards of paperwork for a wartime government that overflowed its offices. Ugly temporary buildings were thrown up on the Mall and barracks-like dormitories were built between the Capitol and Union Station to provide people with working and sleeping space. The dormitories were razed soon after the war but many of the "tempos" remained until very recently.

Peace came in 1918, but thousands of the newcomers stayed. Apartment houses and small homes proliferated in many parts of town, notably on Capitol Hill. "Old Washington vanished, never to return," Mrs. Nicolay mourned. "Its skyline changed from one of dormer windows and aspiring chimneys to the great impersonal apartment houses of tile."

The realities of war and over 100,000 doughboys deaths in the trenches of France killed Wilsonian idealism and created a new isolationism that kept the United States out of the League of Nations. Tired of being exhorted to excellence by a professor-turned-politician, Americans (continued on page 118)

FINAL VICTORY *came after two intense years of effort and sacrifice, marked by such steps as sheep grazing on the White House lawn (above). Opposite below, returning troops march through a specially created arch; opposite above President Wilson, officials and aircraft celebrate the victory on Pennsylvania Avenue in 1919.*

URGENT MEASURES *during the war required the tightening of security and of waist bands. Below, Assistant Secretary of the Navy Franklin D. Roosevelt and others exercise at the White House.*

Capital Sports

Argue as they might about politics or re-development vs restoration of public buildings or the transit system, the one thing Washingtonians agree on is the supremacy of the local sports teams.

Long known as the home of the Washington Senators baseball team, the city was said to be "First in war, first in peace and last in the American League." Those days are long gone — the heritage of Walter Johnson, Harmon Killebrew and Frank Howard was transferred to Texas in 1971. The city mourned the loss, and many in Washington feel that the sports picture in Washington will only be complete when baseball once again returns to the capital.

Meanwhile other sports must take up the slack. The antics of the burgundy-and-gold-clad Washington Redskins, who moved here from Boston in 1937, are of all-consuming interest from the time football training camp starts in July until the very dead of winter. Every Sunday that the Redskins play at home, Robert F. Kennedy Stadium is thronged by ardent fans.

In late fall, as the Redskins are preparing for the divisional play-offs, the Washington's basketball team, the Bullets, are beginning their long season at Capital Center in Largo, Maryland. The Bullets, in their red, white and blue uniforms, have been a Washington team only since 1973, but they quickly became a point of pride and honor in the city.

In 1974 Washington became home-town to a hockey team, the Washington Capitals. Also wearing the patriotic red, white, and blue, the Capitals are already assured of support in this sports-loving city; their Capital Center home will be mobbed.

After the ice has melted, and the basketball standards taken down, Capital Center hosts the green-and-blue clad Maryland Arrows of the National Lacrosse League. This fast paced game is new to the area, but the excitement it generates is catching on. At the same time that box lacrosse is being played at Capital Center, Kennedy Stadium is being used by the Washington Diplomats soccer team. The Diplomats, who also wear red, white and blue uniforms, are helping to increase the already growing interest in this most international of sports.

When the college and club teams of basketball, rugby, football and baseball are added, the Washington sport pages are never wanting for headlines.

PROFESSIONAL SPORTS *hold the attention of many Washingtonians. Below the Washington Bullets demonstrate their special grace; opposite, above the Redskins drive for a touchdown.*

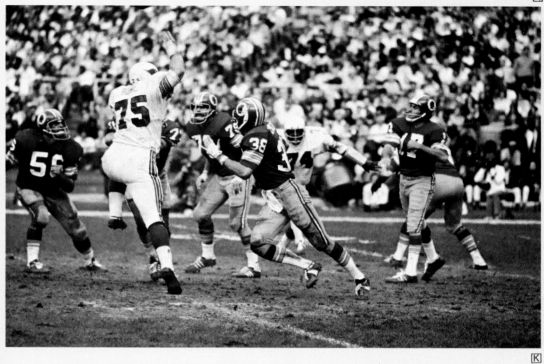

ORGANIZED SPORTS *offer release to Washingtonians young and old. The city, with its Mall, parks and towpaths, offers the perfect setting for invigorating exercise.*

(continued from page 114)

settled for a President willing to ignore good grammar so long as he got his point across. ''Not nostrums but normalcy,'' said Warren G. Harding — and people thought they knew what he meant. Decent and unsuspecting, Harding personified the average middle-class man. His distinguishing trait was his inability to disappoint a friend, a trait which cost his reputation dearly. After his death in office in, 1923 the Teapot Dome debacle became a national shame. But until that scandal broke, few people knew what shenanigans were lining political pockets.

For Washingtonians, the way ''back to normalcy'' was wide open. If the city didn't roar in the 20s, it certainly hummed the tunes of the hometown boy, Al Jolson, and jingled with the sound of money. All kinds of theatres flourished. Keith's still boasted that Wilson had often strolled from the White House to see the likes of Eddie Cantor and Eddie Foy. Oliver Wendell Holmes, one of the most respected Supreme Court jurists of his own or any other day, frequented the Gayety Burlesque. Movie palaces brightened F Street

and Pennsylvania Avenue, N.W. with their flashing marquees, luring patrons to red velveteen and gold painted interiors. The worst single tragedy in Washington history occurred inside such a place. In 1922 a blizzard dropped two feet of snow on the city and caved in the roof of the Knickerbocker Theatre at 18th Street and Columbia Road, N.W. More than 90 moviegoers were killed and another 100 injured.

But by and large, the city was a happy place. It had taken on the proportions of a real city, growing from 278,000 people at the turn of the century to 487,000 by 1930. Fashionable shops along F Street catered to the carriage trade. Cosmopolitan hotels sprang up, for tourism had come into full flower as a major industry. While the new Willard (which replaced the old in 1904) was the most elegant hostelry, it did not lack competition from the Washington Hotel, the Carlton, the Mayflower and the Wardman Park (now the Sheraton Park). During this decade the Cherry Blossom Featival began heralding the tourist season each year.

Visitors added to the capital city's traffic

problem, but ghastly congestion had already seized the city. The growth of government and the automobile's tremendous popularity combined to create a new animal: the commuter who worked downtown but lived in the burgeoning suburbs. Where the Mall was not hidden beneath "tempo" offices, it was blanketed with parked cars. An urban affairs journal of the 1920s noted that the view of Washington from the Virginia approaches "thrust its ugliness upon one's attention with all the insistence of a spoiled child at table." Memorial Bridge briefly eased rush-hour traffic when it linked Arlington with the Mall's end where the Lincoln Memorial sat isolated in a muddy field. But as each new route reached Washington in the course of the next five decades, daily traffic and congestion simply increased and new snarls developed.

Growth further encouraged land speculators, whose free-wheeling tactics prompted belated regulations. Around Piney Branch, a Rock Creek tributary, a critic of urban affairs decried developers who "plastered over the land with the wrong kind of houses set in the wrong kind of lots served by the wrong kind of streets." Fear for the once-charming capital city's future led architects and planners from around the country to make Washington "an inspiring example of sustained interest and intelligent action in city planning." This led to the creation of the National Capital Park and Planning Commission, which coordinates the city's development.

A focal point for improvement, of course, was the federal enclave downtown. One reporter prayed: "May the day come when he who is jealous for the beauty of the national city will not have to shut his eyes as he passes over the great thoroughfare from the Capitol to the Treasury." But the job's enormity was only exceeded by the delays that accompanied its completion. As early as 1910, Congress authorized creation of a Fine Arts Commission to oversee the design and location of all government buildings and monuments. It had met only once and apparently decided, as one wag put it, that putting the old McMillan Plan into effect was "like capturing the Holy City from the infidel."

FROM THE OUTDOOR STALLS *of yesterday (left) to the busy boutiques of today (right) Washington has remained a place where shoppers can delight in the new and different.*

The Fine Arts Commission finally settled down to business during the administration of Calvin Coolidge, whose interest in government building was minimal. Work on the so-called Federal Triangle between slanting Pennsylvania Avenue and straight Constitution Avenue began in 1926 and continued until 1935, largely under the direction of Treasury Secretary Andrew Mellon. The goal was to build new departmental headquarters to accommodate the multiplying numbers of federal employees, with architects designing one building each. The policy brought variety along with curiosities. The Post Office Building, for example, had the largest reception room of any government building including the White House. Because it was constructed on the bed of Tiber Creek, the Commerce Department was built on 15,000 pilings to keep it from sinking. And if these buildings created office space, they did only half the job of realizing Pennsylvania Avenue's ceremonial potential; the north side of the avenue remained a mishmash of dilapidated buildings and disharmonious styles.

By 1929 most Americans were less concerned about lowly skylines (for in Washington the rule is that no building shall rival the Capitol in height) than they were about soaring stock prices and the bull market that was making anybody rich who dared to take a paper gamble. Many felt that the nation was in the midst of a new era and the man who represented the best of it was inaugurated on March 4. "I have no fears for the future of our Country . . . . It is bright with hope," said Herbert Hoover, a former Secretary of Commerce. Eight months later a different era began with a vengeance, as Wall Street crumbled and the depression began.

The blight of depression did not reach here immediately, because Washington was not a center of commerce or finance. The government continued to meet payrolls even when industry could not. President Hoover kept declaring: "Prosperity is just around the corner" but most Americans thought he or the nation was walking backwards. In 1932 the Depression quietly invaded Washington with an army of unemployed World War I veterans. Calling themselves the Bonus Expeditionary Force, they asked Congress to approve immediate payment of a bonus which had been sched-

POOR PEOPLE'S MARCH *of 1968 trouped to the capital city and encamped on soggy ground along the Mall (inset, below).*

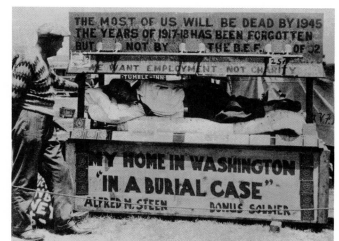

BONUS ARMY MARCHERS *came to Washington in the depths of the Depression to present veterans' petitions. They camped on the Capitol's steps (bottom) and in ingenious "tumble inns" (right).*

CIVIL RIGHTS MARCHERS *rallied to Washington (opposite) in August, 1963 to hear Martin Luther King make his famous address from the Lincoln Memorial (above). Bespeaking an era when all Americans of whatever race might live harmoniously together, he intoned, "I have a dream . . . ."*

GOVERNMENT AGENCIES *spawned like shad in the Potomac during the Depression and war years, confusing some old-time Washingtonians (above).*

uled for 1945. Congress turned a deaf ear. The "army" camped in what were derisively called Hoovervilles: shanty towns on the city's outskirts, notably in relatively open Anacostia near an area commonly used as a dump. Assisted by Washington's Police Superintendent, Pelham D. Glassford, the Bonuseers won high marks for orderly behavior and interracial harmony; their presence was sympathetically accepted by most Washington residents. When Congress refused to pass the Bonus Bill, half the original 20,000 veterans vowed to remain in town — against Presidential and Congressional wishes. Finally, General Douglas MacArthur was called in at the head of a cavalry unit. The veterans were dispersed with tear gas, bayonets and tanks; Washington's orderly but squalid Hoovervilles were burned and bulldozed away. MacArthur believed he had saved the capital; he said his action released "a community . . . held in the grip of a foreign enemy."

The Bonus Army's march signalled the end of what historian Arthur M. Schlesinger, Jr. called "the crisis of the old order."

A new order and the New Deal were ushered in with the inauguration of Franklin D. Roosevelt on March 4, 1933. A cold wind chilled the Capitol Plaza when Roosevelt spoke with the confidence bred of patrician heritage and the proven courage of a man who had prevailed despite the crippling effects of polio. America had "nothing to fear but fear itself," he said. And, as he addressed a nation starving for something to cheer about, the low-lying clouds parted and for a moment the Capitol was bathed in sunlight.

Swiftly the city was inundated with bright young men determined to make the world over. Years later one of those brain-trusters wrote: "We were filled with a vast enthusiasm, although we didn't know exactly for what." Whatever it was, it meant frantic activity. As if to symbolize the new kind of presidency, the President's oval office was moved to its present site at the southeast corner of the White House's west wing. From it emanated an entire lexicon of new government programs and agencies: NRA, AAA, CCC, etc. And dur-

(continued on page 126)

GOVERNMENT HOUSING *had to make room for arriving servicemen and war-time workers (right); also for the Defense Department (at the Pentagon, opposite), and for new departments such as Housing and Urban Development (at L'Enfant Plaza, above).*

A Dazzling Array of Modern Architecture

Post-Civil War Washington saw the development of a new breed of architectural styles. The innovations of Montgomery Meigs Pension Building, called the "Old Red Barn" because of its unique shape and size, were quickly superceded by an even more modern look.

Increasingly the effects of the Parisian school of architecture, L'Ecole des Beaux Arts, made its presence known. In the Kalorama area homes were built according to this style, and increasingly public buildings followed that slick, neo-classical pattern. The architectural firms of McKim, Mead and White, and Carrere and Hastings figured strongly in the architectural styling of turn-of-the-century Washington; both were heavily influenced by the concepts of the Parisian school. Carrere and Hastings's influence can be seen in the Russell Senate Office Building and the Cannon House Office Building. McKim, Mead and White had particular influence on the Mall. The graceful Memorial Bridge and the Reflecting Pool are the statement of their genius.

John Russell Pope, a New York-born architect who also studied in Paris, is probably the best-represented architect in the city.

His works include the Jefferson Memorial, the National Archives, the National Gallery, the National Christian Church and Constitution Hall. Steeped in the tradition of L'Ecole des Beaux Arts, Pope's 20th century works fit in well with Washington's more venerable buildings.

As the European-bred design style continued to gain plaudits, American architecture came into its own. From the architectural schools of Harvard, and M.I.T., Washington increasingly gained a modern look. Though Chinese by birth, Ieoh Ming Pei was trained in the United States. His brilliant structures in the new areas of Southwest Washington just off Independence Avenue stand in dramatic contrast to the more traditional styles of Pope and of McKim, Mead and White. And Edward Durrell Stone, whose works inlcude the interesting National Geographic Building as well as the renowned Kennedy Center, is an architect whose modern elegance is increasingly prevalent in the city. From the purely functional to the exotic, from the traditional to the modern, Washington had expressed the architectural development of the country.

Y

BOLD AND BRILLIANT, *new buildings of glass, steel and concrete transfigure the Washington skyline. The Hilton Hotel, opposite, is on the heights of Connecticut Avenue. The headquarters of the National Geographic Society gleams above. The beauty of the World Health Building (below left) stands apart from the functionalism of the Metro Building (below right).*

(continued from page 123)

ing the 1930s the city's population swelled to 663,000 while the suburbs took shape — or nonshape. The sprawl now so much a part of the region's geography began in earnest. For commuters living in Virginia, new bridges such as Key and the Highway Bridge below 14th Street, became increasingly choked with rush hour traffic. For Marylanders, new spans crossed Rock Creek Valley and developers moved farther out from the city's core.

As the city grew, old problems lingered. The policy of official racial segregation in government offices and public accommodations, which had begun earlier in the century, made life difficult at best for Washington's numerous blacks. By the 1930s blacks were feeling the pinch of residential pressures as well. Local laws prevented them from buying homes in many parts of Maryland and Virginia and a bullish real estate market in the city nudged them from newly chic neighborhoods like Georgetown as white newcomers forced prices up. As a result, many blacks had to move to already overcrowded parts of the city. Later urban renewal programs in

southwest Washington and Capitol Hill would have similar effects; it is only recently that serious consideration has been given to the problems of people displaced by urban renewal.

Meanwhile, the lack of office space was a growing problem for the government. The tiered and columned State, War, Navy Building next to the White House was vastly overcrowded. President Roosevelt urged the building of a single massive new building to house War and Navy; its very size dictated a site outside the city. So, in the 1940s the Pentagon, with its mile-long circumference, rose across the river in Arlington. (FDR wanted it to be a windowless fortress but acquiesced when munitions experts pointed out that windows were needed to withstand any possible explosions.)

The importance of the new defense establishment was made obvious by the increasingly hostile actions of some countries. While Japan belligerantly expanded her "sphere of influence" in the Pacific, Adolph Hitler's mad harangues

POLICE OFFICERS—*from stalwarts of the 1880's (opposite) to a World War I traffic director and modern-day mounties—have helped Washington's visitors and residents survive eras of growth and change.*

G   J

and Benito Mussolini's ranting echoes drowned out feeble cries for peace. The world armed for war again. At first, it seemed the United States might remain a bystander, the "arsenal of democracy." FDR pledged American mothers never to send "our boys to die on foreign soil." But, on December 7, 1941, as Washingtonians flocked to old Griffith Stadium to watch the Redskins face the Philadelphia Eagles, Japanese planes streaked toward the U.S. fleet anchored in Pearl Harbor. Spared the horrifying news while the game progressed, the fans walked out of the stadium into a world at war.

Once again, Washington dressed in khaki and navy blue and legions of people came here to help in the war effort. The housing shortage, was acute, as was the lack of office space. More "tempos" were built; commuters coped with gas rationing by forming car pools. Somehow in the midst of it all, John Russell Pope's design for the Jefferson Memorial became a marble reality beside the Tidal Basin where the fabled cherry trees, a gift from Japan in friendlier times, bloomed beautifully. If

Roosevelt's energetic and experimental economic policies failed to solve the Depression, the war-primed industry eventually ended unemployment. Bread lines were replaced by queued people seeking to buy seeds for Victory Gardens.

Then in the 80th April since Lincoln's death, and with the end of another war in sight, the nation again lost its leader. Roosevelt, the only President ever elected to four terms, died of a stroke less than three months after his last term began. Harry S Truman, who didn't want to be President, told the press after being sworn in: "When they told me . . . what had happened, I felt like the moon, the stars, and all the planets had fallen on me." He soon had a plaque on his desk that read: "The Buck Stops Here." In that spirit "the man from Independence" made many tough decisions and stuck by them.

Controversial but never indecisive, Truman went on to win the Presidency in his own right as voters surprised all the self-appointed experts who predicted New York Governor Thomas E. Dewey would win the 1948 election. But Truman didn't win a

second term in the White House proper; the mansion was discovered to be in a state of structural collapse. Rather than raze the historic house, Truman obtained massive funds to rebuild it from the inside out. The former haberdasher and county judge moved his wife, Bess, his daughter, Margaret, and his beloved piano across the street to Blair House for most of his second term. The White House was rebuilt to gain a grandeur it never had before. When the work was done, the President himself conducted the first televised tour of the building.

In 1947 the State Department vacated what is now the Executive Office Building. But unlike the departments of War and Navy (which were brought together along with the Air Force, as one unit called the Defense Department in that same year), the diplomats stayed within the city limits. Their massive, plain, drab building was constructed in Foggy Bottom, a marginal neighborhood that had been somewhat improved earlier by the relocation of George Washington University from central Washington. While not as bad as erstwhile

Murder Bay, Foggy Bottom once boasted a "free and easy" population, "as full of feuds as the Tennessee mountains." Within twenty-five years this part of town was completely made over. The Kennedy Center was built nearby in 1971. The Watergate apartment and office complex also rose on the Potomac banks, accidentally to achieve unparalleled notoriety.

By the time Dwight D. Eisenhower entered the White House in 1953, the refurbished mansion was the storm center in an increasingly complicated world. Ike installed a putting green on the south lawn and the Oval Office floor still bears the scars of his cleated shoes. "We liked the place," wrote Ike of the White House, "and all it stood for." A Kansas farm boy who went to West Point and on from there to become Supreme Allied Commander in WW II, he was a career soldier who accepted a general's pension benefits rather than a President's on his retirement. He took more interest in historic Gettysburg, Pennsylvania, where he and Mamie built a home, than in the capital city. But his interest in, and support for, the National Highway Act

RIOTS OF 1968 *damaged many blocks of the city, particularly in black residential sections.*

had enormous effects on Washington. By enabling Americans to travel longer distances over high speed roads, it increased tourism in the capital city. It also encouraged the expansion of suburban development, often at the expense of inner-city businesses and neighborhoods.

From a 1950 high of 802,000 people, the District of Columbia's population dropped to 756,000 in 20 years, while the metropolitan area's population nearly doubled to top 2,500,000. The circular Beltway, which rings the city ten miles from its center, became "the main street of Washington." Partially to avoid worsening the already frightful traffic congestion, many government agencies moved out of town. The National Institutes of Health expanded into nearby Maryland. The Atomic Energy Commission, the National Bureau of Standards, the Census Bureau and the Central Intelligence Agency all went out to the countryside. Planners saw the dangers of this explosion; by 1968 a new policy was established, 60 percent of the government work force would be employed in the District and 40 percent out of town.

(continued on page 133)

RENEWAL AREAS *have bloomed in many parts of Washington, including 14th Street (top) and Sherman Avenue in the northwest section (above).*

129

Washington's Ethnic Diversity

For many reasons — because it was not a major port city, because it was not a way station to the vast farmlands of the middle-west, because it never developed as an industrial city — Washington did not develop or attract ethnic groupings. From the very start most of the population here was either black or white. Yet some interesting ethnic groupings have always existed. While canal and railroad work was in progress many Irish lived in the city, and the German community was well known for its breweries in the latter half of the nineteenth century. Around the beginning of the twentieth century a sizeable Italian community existed in the Brookland area of Northeast Washington. These ethnic groupings have diminished in recent years and been replaced by others.

Washington's Chinatown, small in comparison to those of New York or San Francisco is, nevertheless, an area of great interest to residents and tourists. According to local legends, the first Chinese family appeared in Washington around 1851 and moved into an attractive home near 3rd Street on Pennsylvania Avenue. In the decades that followed, others appeared, and by 1880 Washington had a thriving Chinese community that extended from the base of Capitol Hill up to about 4th Street along Pennsylvania Avenue. The community was disrupted by the development of the Federal Triangle area in the 1920's and '30's and gradually moved northward to its present location on H Street. Present-day Chinatown occupies several blocks along H Street, with the greatest concentration from about 5th to 7th Streets. Numerous excellent Chinese restaurants flourish in the area. And although there are at most 500 residents in Chinatown, the New Year's celebration is an event of great interest to Washingtonians.

More recently established than the Chinese section, the Hispanic community in the Adams-Morgan area of the city has grown rapidly in the past decade. With its greatest concentration in the area of 18th and Columbia Road, N.W., the community now numbers in excess of 30,000. The residents come from several countries including El Salvador, Cuba and Guatemala, and have added their pan-American style and diversity to the city. Restaurants featuring Latin-American food have sprung up, as have Spanish language newspapers and a movie theatre specializing in films in Spanish. The local elementary school teaches all courses in both Spanish and English and draws a number of English speaking students who hope to learn a new language early. Because of its size, the Hispanic community is not so tightly knit as that of Chinatown, but community organizations and meeting places are adding to the sense of togetherness.

With diplomats from foreign lands and embassy employees in native garb a common sight, Washington has indeed an exotic flavor. And while our city does not boast the ethnic mix of New York or Chicago it is proud of its cosmopolitan nature.

WASHINGTON IS HOME *to many nationalities. A summer in the parks program, in Farragut Square (below), a canal side lecture (above left), a celebration in Lafayette Square and a Pan-American gathering in the Adams-Morgan area (right) demonstrate the city's diversity.*

CONGRESSMEN AND CABINET MEM-
BERS *find time in busy schedules to
meet with constituents young and old. At
left, the Capitol provides an imposing
backdrop for Texas Congressman J. J.
Pickle. Below, Interior Secretary Rogers
C. B. Morton and Maryland Congressman Gilbert Gude share a joke with
youngsters.*

(continued from page 129)

Though this meant a spurt of suburban building, new areas within the city still rose, like the new Department of Housing and Urban Development, the gleaming blocks along Independence Avenue, and a new House office building, named for longtime Speaker Sam Rayburn. Upon completion, it was said to be the most expensive office structure ever built. It is also, perhaps, the most imposing, though no responsible critic has accused it of being the most beautiful.

Before his death President John F. Kennedy brought a renewed liveliness to official Washington and reawakened interest in Pennsylvania Avenue as a ceremonial street. But it was his successor, Lyndon B. Johnson, who reorganized the District government while Lady Bird pursued a national beautification program that left the city blooming with flowers.

Recently, Congress passed legislation that allows local residents to elect their own Mayor and City Council. Though Congress still holds certain veto powers, Washington's city government is no longer a "monster with 50 heads, snapping at one another" or "an ingenious system of committees which veto each other's recommendations." "Home Rule for the Last Colony" is becoming a reality before the 200th birthday of the nation that gave democracy to the modern world.

The strength of that democracy, and the importance of Washington as a symbol of it, was never more strikingly displayed than during the last difficult days of the Watergate crisis. The great powers of the Presidency shifted to Gerald R. Ford and the nation and the world looked to Washington for assurances that our way of life would be continued and our commitments upheld.

Thus Washington's importance is ever growing, serving as a mirror of the nation it leads. Rural when the country was agricultural, increasingly urban since the turn of the century, Washington's problems and advantages have changed with the passage of time. The crush of automobile traffic forced alterations in the way of life, but the coming of the Metro subway system will offer a substitute for the car. Perhaps the city has not yet fulfilled its aristocratic planners' grand dreams, but it is, nonetheless, a truly American city, alive with adventure, with things to do and see. Eagerly awaiting the Bicentennial, Washington looks back on her past with rightful pride.

LIKE A SUNBURST, *fireworks light the monument to the city's namesake; in the distance, the Capitol, symbol of the city's purpose, glows through the night.*

WASHINGTON'S METRO, a 96-mile subway and elevated rapid transit system (see map), will open in 1976 to relieve such automobile-induced congestion as the scene below of cars pouring off Key Bridge into Georgetown. At left a mason—one of thousands of workers involved in the 10-year project—puts a final tile in place.

Ⓗ

Ⓓ

AT FUTURE STATIONS, *architects envision a blending of styles to please both traditional and modern-minded Metro riders.*

AT NATIONAL AIRPORT *cars on an elevated track will carry arriving passengers to the city's heart in nine minutes.*

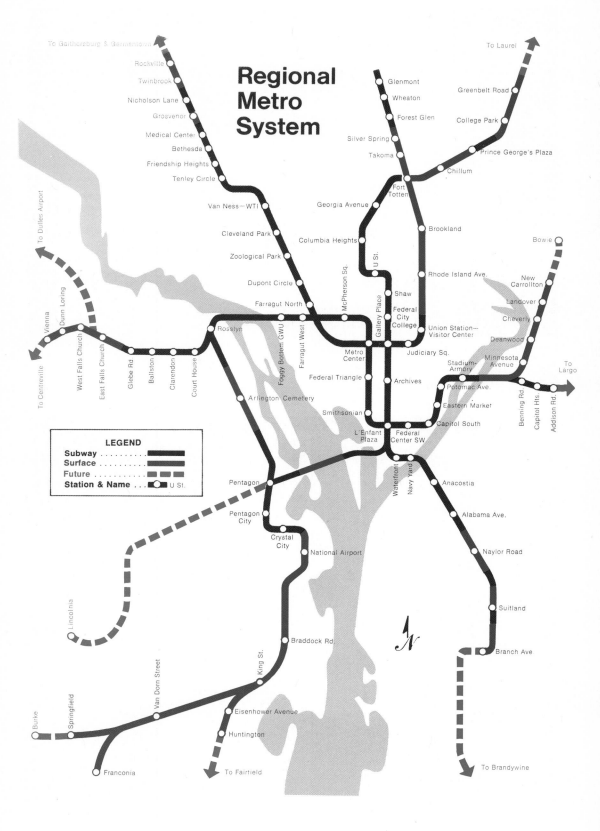

Regional Metro System

LEGEND
- Subway . . . .
- Surface . . . .
- Future . . . .
- Station & Name . . . ○ U St.

To Gaithersburg & Germantown
Rockville
Twinbrook
Nicholson Lane
Grosvenor
Medical Center
Bethesda
Friendship Heights
Tenley Circle
Van Ness—WTI
Cleveland Park
Zoological Park
Dupont Circle
Farragut North
Rosslyn
West Falls Church
East Falls Church
Glebe Rd.
Ballston
Clarendon
Court House
To Dulles Airport
To Centreville
Vienna
Dunn Loring
Arlington Cemetery
Pentagon
Pentagon City
Crystal City
National Airport
Lincolnia
Braddock Rd.
Burke
Springfield
Van Dorn Street
King St.
Eisenhower Avenue
Huntington
Franconia
To Fairfield

McPherson Sq.
Foggy Bottom GWU
Farragut West
Federal Triangle
Smithsonian
L'Enfant Plaza
Metro Center
Gallery Place
Archives
Federal Center SW
Waterfront
Navy Yard

Glenmont
Wheaton
Forest Glen
Silver Spring
Takoma
Georgia Avenue
Columbia Heights
U St.
Shaw
Federal City College
Union Station—Visitor Center
Judiciary Sq.
Fort Totten
Brookland
Rhode Island Ave.
Chillum
Capitol South
Eastern Market
Potomac Ave.
Stadium-Armory
Anacostia
Alabama Ave.
Naylor Road
Suitland
Branch Ave.
To Brandywine

To Laurel
Greenbelt Road
College Park
Prince George's Plaza
Bowie
New Carrollton
Landover
Cheverly
Deanwood
Minnesota Avenue
Benning Rd.
Capitol Hts.
Addison Rd.
To Largo

Walking Tour of Capitol Hill

Sunny days anytime of year offer visitors a perfect chance to savor the full flavor of Washington by taking a walking tour. Capitol Hill with its varied architecture, sculpture and shops provides one of the city's most interesting tours. A tour of the hill takes a full day and provides many insights into the Washington way of life.

Starting at the southeast base of the hill, the walker can visit the beautiful, and aromatic Botanic Gardens — just across Independence Avenue from the gardens is the elegant fountain designed by Frederick Bartholdi, who designed the Statue of Liberty in New York. West of the Botanic Gardens stands the massive Grant memorial, the largest statuary grouping in Washington. The numerous figures in this grouping are capped by the equestrian figure of General Grant, the largest equestrian figure in the United States, and next to that of Victor Emmanuel in Rome, the largest in the world.

If the day is warm, a restful stop can be made at the rustic spring grotto on the west front terraces of the Capitol. The grotto, part of famed landscape architect Frederick Olmsted's plan for the west front grounds now with city water in its fountains, originally offered cool spring water for the thirsty. Looking up Capitol Hill, the Capitol Building rises — majestically fulfilling L'Enfant's prediction that Jenkins Hill was "a pedestal awaiting a monument."

The walk up Constitution Avenue, with the Capitol on the right and the Russell and Dirksen Senate Office Buildings on the left is the ceremonial route taken by Presidents after the inauguration ceremonies on the Capitol's East Front Plaza. Facing the Capitol on 1st Street and Maryland Avenue is the austere Supreme Court Building. Erected on the site of the temporary "Old Brick Capitol," it contains in addition to the judge's chambers and court room, a massive law library and halls filled with interesting displays.

Directly behind the Supreme Court Building is A Street, N.E. A narrow, typical residential street of Capitol Hill, the houses here date from the latter half of the 19th and early 20th centuries. Of particular interest is the town house of Frederick Douglass at 316 A Street. Now the Museum of African Art, Douglass's home was built in 1870 and demonstrates a style quite common in the time. Further up A Street are row houses and apartment buildings that were constructed after WW I built to house "war workers" who decided to make Washington their permanent home.

A pleasant walk south along 7th Street continues the tour of Capitol Hill. Wide East Capitol Street, with large bay-fronted townhouses and busy Independence Avenue with its older homes provide interesting contrasts. The walk along 7th Street ends at Eastern Market at 7th & C Streets, S.E. Outdoor stalls with fresh produce brought in from nearby farms enliven the scene around the Grant era market on Saturdays. Inside, the many stalls offer a refreshing change from today's impersonal super markets.

The hungry visitor can now take a pleasant walk west down Pennsylvania Avenue, the "main street" of Capitol Hill. Little restaurants, and interesting shops and street vendors give this part of Pennsylvania Avenue a feel that is much like Georgetown. After a quiet lunch, the tour continues down Pennsylvania Avenue.

Independence and Pennsylvania Avenues meet at 2nd Street, S.E. where the massive Library of Congress Building and the two Library Annexes dominate the scenery. The main building with its impressive reading room and numerous murals and statuary, is second home to many of our nation's scholars. Just north of the Library, at the corner of 2nd and East Capitol Street is the Folger Shakespeare Library. Set off by the intriguing statue of Puck, the Folger is the largest library in the world devoted solely to the Elizabethan Age.

Returning to the base of Capitol Hill by way of Independence Avenue, the visitor passes the three House office buildings: the Cannon, the Longworth, and the Rayburn. To the right the south side of the Capitol and the rolling Capitol grounds complete the view of the building that is a "monument to democracy."

A CITY of "Magnificent distances," Washington is a great town for walkers In addition, to Capitol Hill, tours of Lafayette Square and the Canal area offer interesting diversion.

Driving Tour

Years before President Washington and Congress decided where to place the capital of our nation, this area was popular with planters who found the rich soil and navigable waterways perfect for development of cash crops. Many of the homes built by these planters are now open to the public. A day-long, driving tour of the Washington area provides an opportunity to see three of the most interesting homes as well as a Colonial tavern, a major fortress on the Potomac and the rugged terrain around the fall line at Great Falls, Maryland.

As the early morning sun glistens on the rushing waters of Great Falls, the tour begins. The Falls, which are reached by taking the Maryland Beltway and following the signs, clearly reveal the terrain that early planners saw when they chose this spot as the Capital. Beside the river, the placid canal with its towpaths and canal inn (now a museum) shows how our ancestors struggled to alter the land to fit their purposes.

A beautiful drive down George Washington Memorial Parkway to Alexandria brings the tourist to one of the two colonial towns, the other being Georgetown, in the original ten-mile square federal district. Here, at 128 North Royal Street stands Gadsby's Tavern and City Hotel. The tavern, the smaller of the two buildings, was frequented by George Washington and, in fact, was his first military headquarters (in 1754) and the site of his last military appearance (in 1798). Gadsby's old brick walls were the silent witnesses to much of our early history.

As the visitor returns to the George Washington Parkway, the next scene is of old Alexandria with its restored colonial homes and rough cobblestone streets. Thereafter the driver can easily reach one of America's true historic shrines, Mount Vernon, by means of a pleasant route along the Potomac and through the fertile Virginia countryside.

Mount Vernon, with its white columns and rolling lawns is a part of every American's childhood. Built in the early 1750's and designed in part by our first President, it was his point of origin, and the place to which he sought to return. At one time in danger of collapse, the beautiful home and gardens restored by the Mount Vernon Ladies Association are worth a trip to Washington by themselves.

On U.S. Route 1, not far from Mount Vernon — once part of Washington's estate — stands the graceful Woodlawn Plantation. The mansion was designed by the ubiquitous William Thornton in 1800, although George Washington had deeded the lands to his nephew many years earlier, as a wedding gift. With its solid appearance, and manicured lawns, Woodlawn typifies tidewater Virginia plantations.

The last of the three major mansions on the tour is the famed Gunston Hall. Not far from Mount Vernon, Gunston Hall is on Virginia Route 242 near Lorton. George Mason, whose great interest in civil liberties is reflected in our Bill of Rights, was the first owner of this interesting

house. Built about the time of Mount Vernon its restrained but elegant interiors and gardens offer good contrasts with the architecture preferred by George Washington. Together the two demonstrate domestic building styles popular in mid-18th century Virginia.

The driving tour ends with a trip to the only real fortress in the Washington area, Fort Washington. On the Maryland side of the Potomac, almost opposite Mount Vernon, the fort is reached by taking the beltway to Maryland Route 210, Indian Head Highway, and going south until signs to Fort Washington appear. The site for Fort Washington was chosen by our first President and the massive fortress was completed in time for service in the war of 1812. Unfortunately, the fort did not fulfill its function as defender of the city during that war. Instead, the fort was destroyed at the hands of the American defenders. Now under the auspices of the National Park Service, the fort's great battlements provide perfect climbing places for children, and the huge shade trees and large green spaces make it perfect for picnics and cookouts.

The driving tour ends at Fort Washington, but the sense of having stepped back into the city's past remains, as does the satisfying feeling of having touched the history of our country.

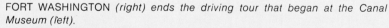

FORT WASHINGTON *(right) ends the driving tour that began at the Canal Museum (left).*

Index

Bibliography

Lonnelle Aikman, *We, the People: The Story of the United States Capitol Its Past and Its Promise,* (Washington: United States Capitol Historical Society, 1974) 144 pp.

Lonnelle Aikman and Frank Freidel, George Washington Man And Monument, (Washington: Washington National Monument Association, 1973) 72 pp.

Emily E. Briggs, *The Olivia Letters* (New York: The Neale Publishing Company, 1906) 445 pp.

Letitia Brown, *Free Negroes in the District of Columbia 1790-1846* (New York: Oxford University Press, 1972) 146 pp.

Wilhelms Bogart Bryan, *History of the National Capitol* (New York: Macmillian Company, 1916) 2 vols.

Mary Cable, *Avenue of the Presidents* (Boston: Houghton Mifflin Company, 1969)

Elizabeth S. Kite, *L'Enfant and Washington* (Baltimore: John Hopkins Press, 1929) 182 pp. Bibliography.

Constance McLaughlin Green, *Washington* (Princeton: Princeton University Press, 1963) 2 vols.

Constance McLaughlin Green, *Secret City* (Princeton: Princeton University Press, 1967) 289 pp.

Frederick Gutheim, *The Potomac* (New York and Toronto: Rinehart and Company, Inc., 1946), 436 pp.

Mary Anne Harrell and Stuart E. Jones. *Equal Justice Under The Law: The Supreme Court In American Life* (Washington: The Foundation of the Federal Bar Association, 1965) 144 pp.

Margaret Leech, *Reveille In Washington, 1860-1865* (New York and London: Harper and Brothers, 1941) 483 pp.

Helen Nicolay, *Our Capitol on the Potomac* (New York and London: Century Company, 1924) 545 pp.

James Whyte, *The Uncivil War: Washington During Reconstruction 1865-1878* (New York: Wayne Press, 1953) 316 pp.

James Sterling Young, *The Washington Community, 1800-1828* (New York: Columbia University Press, 1966) 307 pp.

Key to Pictorial Matter

Pictorial matter for this volume has been drawn from a number of institutions to which the editors are profoundly grateful. Throughout the book, symbols under each picture mark its source as shown in the listing below.

[A] American Antiquarian Society
[B] Brazilian Embassy
[C] Columbia Historical Society
[D] District of Columbia Redevelopment Land Agency
[E] Department of Defense
[F] Embassy of Japan
[G] Library of Congress
[H] Metro
[I] National Archives
[J] National Capital Park Service
[K] National Football League
[L] National Gallery, Washington, D.C.
[M] National Geographic Society

[N] National Museum, Stockholm
[O] National Park Service
[P] National Portrait Gallery
[Q] New York Historical Society
[R] New York Public Library
[S] Pennsylvania Academy of Fine Arts
[T] Shirley L. Green
[U] Smithsonian Institution
[V] Society of the Cincinnatus
[W] Supreme Court
[X] Washington Convention & Visitors Bureau
[Y] Washington Hilton Hotel
[Z] White House

Map Index

Adas Israel Synagogue (F-8)
3rd & G Street, N.W.
Being made into museum of Jewish history.

American University
Mass & Nebraska Ave., N.W.
The city's youngest university.

Anacostia Neighborhood Museum
2405 Martin Luther King Ave.
Mon.-Fri. 10-6:00 Weekends 1-6:00

Andrew Jackson Statue (F-6)
Lafayette Park

Aquatic Gardens
Kenilworth & Douglas St., N.E.
A beautiful place in late summer.
Daily 8-sundown

Arlington National Cemetery
The major national cemetery; final resting place of John F. and Robert F. Kennedy.
Daily April-Oct. 8-7:00 Nov.-Mar. 8-5:00

Arena Kreeger Stages (I-8)
6th & M Street, S.W.
Home of Washington's Repertory Theatre.

The Arts Club (James Monroe House) (F-5)
2017 I Street, N.W.
Owner-builder, Timothy Caldwell, was forced to sell it shortly after completion.
Mon., Tues., Thurs., Fri. 11-5:00
Wed. 2-5:00 Weekends: 1-5:00

Bartholdi Fountain (H-9)
2nd & Independence, S.W.
Designed and cast in Paris.

Benjamin Stoddert House (E-2)
3400 Prospect Ave., N.W.
Constructed by Washington's Secretary of the Navy.

Blair-Lee Mansion (F-6)
1650 Pennsylvania Ave., N.W.
Here, in 1950, that the attempt on Truman's life occurred.

Botanic Gardens (H-9)
Independence & First, S.W.
This institution will identify any unusual plants sent to it.
Daily except Saturday 9-5:00 Free

Bureau of Printing and Engraving (H-6)
14th & C St., S.W.
This is where the paper money of America is printed. 8:00-2:30

Canal Lock House (G-6)
17th & Constitution, N.W.
A reminder that in the early years Constitution Avenue was a canal.

Dolley Madison House (F-6)
21 Madison Place, N.W.

Dumbarton Oaks
3101 R Street, N.W.
Scene of an important WW II conference. Excellent collection of pre-Columbia art is on the grounds.
Hours: House—Tues.-Sunday 2-4:45
Gardens—Daily 2-4:45

Eastern Market (H-10)
7th & C Street, S.E.
Built in 1872, it is the only municipal market operating. Mon.-Sat.: 8-6:00

Embassy Row
Massachusetts Ave., bet. Connecticut and Wisconsin Avenues.

Executive Office Building (F-6)
(old State War Navy Bldg.)
Pennsylvania & 17th, N.W.
An example of Gilded Age gaudiness.

FBI Building (G-7)
Pennsylvania Ave., bet. 7th & 8th
Interesting tours available.
9:15-4:15

Federal City College (F-6)
1420 New York Ave. N.W.
School is gaining an excellent reputation.

Folger Library (G-10)
201 East Capitol St., S.E.
Dedicated to Shakespeare and things Elizabethan. Mon.-Sat.: 10:00-4:30
Sun.: 12-4:30

Fords Theatre (F-7)
511 10th St., N.W.
Lincoln was assassinated here. Lincoln museum in basement.

Fort McNair
Greenleaf's Point S.W. Washington
Home of the Army War College, one of the country's oldest military establishments.

Franciscan Monastery
14th & Quincy St., N.E.
Monday-Saturday 8:30-4:00

Frederick Douglass Memorial Home
(Cedar Hill) 1411 W. St., S.E.
Less gaudy Victorian architecture.
Mon.-Fri.: 9-4:00 Sat.-Sun : 10-5:00

Freer Gallery (H-7)
12th & Jefferson Drive, S.W.
Contains an enormous collection of orientalia and country's major collection of Whistler. Daily 10-5:30

John Marshall House (F-5)
1801 F Street, N.W.
This house has been occupied by John Marshall, Presidents Madison and Van Buren, and Major General McClellan.

L'Enfant Plaza (H-7)
Southside Independence Ave. at 9th-12th.
The Plaza includes many shops.

Library of Congress (H-9)
1st & Independence Ave., S.E.
A good example of neo-French Renaissance design.
Mon.-Fri.: 8:30 a.m.-9:30 p.m.
Sat.: 8:30-5:00 Sun.: 10-5:00

Lightship "Chesapeake"
Haines Point, off Ohio Drive
October-May Saturday-Sunday 1-4:00

Lincoln Memorial (G-4)
West end of Mall
Probably the most visited memorial in the world. Daily: 8-Midnight

Luther Place Memorial Church (E-6)
Vermont Ave. at Thomas Circle N.W.
Stained glass windows depict reformers in the Protestant movements of Europe.

Museum of African Art (H-10)
316 A Street, N.E.
The 1st Washington home of Frederick Douglass, ex-slave, American statesman.
Mon.-Fri.: 11-5:00 Weekends: 12:30-5:00

National Air and Space Museum (H-7)
bet. 9th & 7th on Jefferson Drive
Daily 10-5:30 (summer hours longer)

National Arboretum
Bladensburg Rd. & R St., N.E.
April-October: 8-7:00 Nov.-Mar.: Mon.-Fr.: 8-5:00 Weekends: 10-5:00

National Archives (G-7)
8th & Constitution, N.W.
Declaration and Constitution, are on view.
Oct.-Mar.: Mon.-Sat.: 9-6:00 Apr.-Sept.: Mon.-Sat.: 9-10:00 Sun. 1-10:00 p.m.

National Cathedral
Wisconsin & Mass. Avenue, N.W.
Still under construction.

National City Christian Church (E-6)
14th at Thomas Circle, N.W.
American colonial churches recalled here.

National Gallery of Art (G-8)
6th & Constitution Ave., N.W.
One of the most complete in the world.
Mon.-Sat.: 10-9:00 Sun.: 12-9:00

Phillips Gallery
21st & P St., N.W.
A turn-of-the-century brownstone houses one of the great private art collections.
Tues.-Sat.: 10-5:00 Sunday: 2-7:00

Post Office (tower) (G-7)
1200 Pennsylvania Ave., N.W.
Example of Romanesque Revival architecture.

Post Office Department (G-7)
Pennsylvania Ave. bet. 11th & 12th
Its gracefully curved facade opens onto an attractive court-yard.

Renwick Gallery (F-6)
17th & Penn Ave., N.W.
One of the first major buildings in something other than Greek revival style in the city. Daily 10-5:30

Robert F. Kennedy Stadium
22nd & East Capitol, S.E.

Rock Creek Cemetery
Rock Creek Church Rd., N.W.
Contains August St. Gaudens statue "Grief"

Rock Creek Park (E-4)
Along Rock Creek
Follows the path of Rock Creek through the District and four miles into Maryland.

Saint Sophia Catheral (B-2)
36th & Mass Ave., N.W.
The architecture is modified Byzantine.

Senate Office Buildings (G-9)
Constitution Ave. bet. Delaware Avenue and 2nd St., N.E.

Shrine of the Immaculate Conception
Mich. & 4th St., N.E.
The Shrine is the largest Catholic Church in the United States and the 7th largest church in the world.

Smithsonian Institute (H-7)
Jefferson Dr. bet. 9th & 12th, S.W.
The "Red Sandstone Castle" was designed by James Renwick. Daily: 10-5:30

Society of Cincinnati
(Lars Anderson House) 2118 Mass. Ave., N.W.
Attractive turn of the century house.
Monday-Saturday 2-4:00

St. Johns Church (F-6)
16th & H St., N.W.
Benjamin Henry Latrobe was so pleased with his design that he served for several years as the organist there.

State Department (G-5)
23rd & C Street, N.W.

Supreme Court (G-9)
1st and East Capitol Street, S.E.
Austere design allows effective use of displays in the corridors. Mon.-Fri. 9:30-4:00

Sylvan Theatre (H-6)
Base of Washington Monument Grounds
Used primarily during the summer for performances of Shakespearean plays.

Tariff Commission (G-7)
(old Post Office) bet. 7th & 8th on E St., N.W.
Along with the Patent Office, the construction of the post office in the 1830's made the area a focus of activity.

Textile Museum
2320 S Street, N.W.
Tues.-Sat.: 10-5:00

Theodore Roosevelt Island
South of Key Bridge, enter Virginia side.
Daily: 9:30-sundown

Tudor Place
1644 31st St., N.W.
Represents a significant break with the Georgian architecture of the preceding century.

Union Station (F-9)
at Mass. and Louisiana, N.W.
This Roman classical building is soon to become the National Visitors Center.

Washington Monument (G-6)
The Mall
At 555 feet this monument was the tallest in the world at the time of its completion.
8:00-12 mid. Labor Day-Mar. 18: 9-5:00

Waterfront (I-7)
Maine Ave., S.W.

Watergate Apartment Complex (F-4)
Rock Creek Pkwy. & Va. Avenue
Includes an interesting shopping mall.

Wax Museum (E-8)
5th & K Street, N.W.
Contains representatives of people and events important to American and biblical history. Daily: 9-8:00

White House (F-6)
1600 Pennsylvania Avenue
Tues.-Sat. 10-12:00

Willard Hotel (G-6)
14th & Pennsylvania Ave., N.W.
One of the most glamorous hotels in the city in its day.

Woodrow Wilson Home
2340 S Street, N.W.
Daily: 10-4:00

National Geographic Society (E-6)
17th & M Streets, N.W.
Edward Durrell Stone's first building in Washington, Contains Explorer's Hall.
Mon.-Fri.:9-6:00 Sat.: 9-5:00 Sun.::12-5:00

National Museum of History & Tech. (G-7)
Constitution Ave. bet. 12th & 14th, N.W.
The museum houses fascinating collections of all types of Americana.
Daily 10-5:30 (summer hours longer)

National Portrait Gallery (F-7)
(old Patent Office) bet. 7th & 9th on G St., N.W.
Its collection of portraits of Americans is unique. Daily: 10:00-5:30

National Theatre (F-7)
1321 E Street, N.W.
The oldest theatre in Washington.

National Women's Party (G-10)
(Sewell-Belmont House) 2nd & Constitution Ave., N.E.
One of the oldest homes in the city. Tours by appointment only.

National Zoological Park
3001 Connecticut Ave., N.W.
Daily: Summer—9-6:00 Winter—9-4:30

Navy Yard (J-10)
8th & M Street, S.E.
Excellent museum on its grounds.
Museum: Weekdays: 9-4:00 Weekends: 10-5:00

New York Ave. Presbyterian Church (F-7)
1313 New York Avenue N.W.

Octagon House (F-5)
18th & New York Avenue, N.W.
One of the best examples of Federal architecture in the city.
Tues.-Sat.: 10-4:00 Sunday: 1-4:00

Old Pension Building (F-8)
5th & G Street, N.W.
The frieze depicts aspects of life in the Union Army.

Old Stone House
3051 M Street, N.W.
The oldest extant house in Georgetown, stone construction. Daily 9:30-5:00

Organization of American States (G-6)
(Pan American Building) Constitution & 17th St., N.W.
An excellent example of Spanish colonial style architecture. Mon.-Sat.: 8:30-4:00

Peterson House (F-7)
(where Lincoln died) 516 10th St., N.W.
The government bought this house in 1896.
Daily: 9-5:00

Gallaudet College
Corner West Virginia on Florida Ave., N.E.
The first college for the deaf in the world.

George Washington University (F-5)
bet. Virginia & Pennsylvania Avenue, 20th & 23rd Sts., N.W.
Recent additions include a library and a student union building.

Georgetown University
Western portion of Georgetown off 37th Street & Reservoir Road, N.W.
The Healy Building, by architects of the Library of Congress, Smithmeyer & Pelz.

Government Printing Office (F-9)
North Capitol bet. G & H Sts.
The largest printing establishment in America. Monday-Friday: 8-4:00

Grant Memorial (G-9)
1st & Pennsylvania Ave., N.W.
Symbolizes and memorializes Grant's importance in the saving of the Union.

Henderson Marine Barracks
9th bet. G & H Sts.
The oldest Marine Corps post in America. Parades in Summer, May-September 9:00

Hirshhorn Museum (H-7)
7th & Jefferson Dr., S.W.
The unusual shape allows for effective displays inside and out. 10-5:30

Hispanic Community
Adams Morgan Area N.W.
Columbia & 18th Street
An especially good place for Latin food.

House Office Building (H-9)
Independence Ave. bet. 1st St., S.W. and I Street, S.E.

Howard University
7th St. & Georgia Ave. & 4th St. bet. W and Gresham Place
Founders Library the most complete library of Negro Americana in the world.

Islamic Center
The Center was designed by the Egyptian Ministry of Endowment to conform with Arab and Islamic architecture. Daily: 10-4:00

Jefferson Memorial (I-6)
Tidal Basin S.W. Washington
Designed by John R. Pope, this memorial received mixed reviews. Daily 8-12 midnight Summer Band Concerts: 8:30 p.m.

John F. Kennedy Center for the Performing Arts (F-4) 2700 F Street, N.E.
Daily: 10-9:00

Capitol (G-9)
Capitol Hill
Daily: 9-4:30 Summer Band Concerts: 8:00

Catholic University
4th & Michigan Ave., N.E.
Pres. Cleveland witnessed cornerstone laying in 1888.

Chinatown (F-8)
H between 5th & 7th Sts., N.W.

Christian Heurich Mansion (E-5)
20th & New Hampshire Ave.
Home of the Columbia Historical Society.
Monday, Wednesday, Saturday: 10-4:00

Church of the Latter Day Saints
2810 16th St., N.W.
The design of this Mormon Church reflects the Tabernacle in Salt Lake City, Utah.

Columbus Fountain (F-9)
Union Station Plaza

Congressional Cemetery
1801 E Street, S.E.
It contains the remains of John Sousa and Mathew Brady.

Corcoran Gallery (G-6)
17th & E St., N.W.
Example of Beaux-Arts tradition at its best.
Tues.-Sun. 11-5:00

Curtis Lee Mansion
Arlington National Cemetery
A mansion in the Greek revival tradition, designed by George Hadfield.
Oct.-Mar.: 9:30-4:30 Apr.-Sept.: 9:30-6:00

D.C. Courthouse (old City Hall) (G-8)
4th & D Street, N.W.
Designed by George Hadfield.

D.C. Teachers College
Harvard Between 13th & 14th Streets.

Decatur House (F-6)
H & Jackson St., N.W.
The first house built on Lafayette Square.
Mon.-Sun. 10:30-4:00

Department of Agriculture (H-7)
14th & Independence, S.W.
Under construction longer than any other executive department building.

Department of Commerce (G-6)
14th & Constitution Ave., N.W.
Includes census clock on first floor, aquarium in the basement. Daily: 9-5:00

Department of Justice (G-7)
9th & Pennsylvania, N.W.

District Building (G-7)
E Street at 14th
One of Washington's best examples of Parisian Beaux-Arts architecture.

144